appetizers

a dierbergs school of cooking publication

Appetizers
A Dierbergs School of Cooking Publication

Copyright 2009
Dierbergs Markets, Inc.
16690 Swingley Ridge Road
Chesterfield, Missouri 63017

This cookbook is a collection of recipes which has been developed and tested by Dierbergs Home Economists.

ISBN: 978-0-9749955-5-7
First Printing 2009

Cover photograph:
Tomato Bacon Mini Tarts
Recipe on page 54

Acknowledgements

Director of Marketing and Advertising
John Muckerman

Managing Editor
Gena Bast

Food Editor
Barb Ridenhour

Cookbook Project Manager
Janice Martin

Copywriter
Therese Lewis

Art Director/Designer
Mike Parker

Dierbergs School of Cooking Managers
Sally Bruns, Loretta Evans, Ginger Gall, Jennifer Kassel, Nancy Lorenz

Photographer
Steve Adams, Steve Adams Studio

Food Stylist
Carol Ziemann

Food Styling Assistant
Janice Martin

Prop Stylist
Karen Hurych

Nutrition Analysis
Trish Farano, DTR, Dierbergs Markets
Sherri Hoyt, RD, LD, Missouri Baptist Medical Center

Recipe Editing
Patty Tomaselli

Contributors
Chef Coby Arzola, Mary Billings, Cathy Chipley, Greg and Sue Dierberg, Sharon Dierberg, Karen Hurych, Laura Dierberg Padousis, Nancy Raben, Linda Walton, Carol Ziemann

TABLE OF
contents

10

64

26

78

46

84

"I love entertaining family and friends, planning the menu, setting the table, adding personal touches and watching everything come together. I hope this book helps you create delicious beginnings and wonderful memories. Enjoy!"

– Sharon Dierberg

Introduction

Whether carefully planned or spur-of-the-moment, nothing says *party* quite like an array of tempting appetizers. Little bites with big flavors are at the center of today's relaxed style of entertaining.

Inviting people over for appetizers and drinks has a timeless appeal that lets everyone mix, mingle, and savor wonderful food with great conversation. Who can resist the temptation to graze on a platter of cheese and crackers, a bowl of crunchy nuts, or a tray of freshly-baked savory delights wrapped in pastry?

It's your turn to be the host, so send out the invitations. Then start paging through this book. You'll find all sorts of stylish starters from Dierbergs School of Cooking to create the perfect gathering. Impress your guests with Beautiful Raspberry Brie (page 15), Tandoori Chicken Bites (page 41), or Tomato Bacon Mini Tarts (page 54). Kick back and dip into Caramelized Onion and Gorgonzola Dip (page 72) while you sip on White Zinfandel Lemonade Slush (page 82).

Whether it's a casual get-together or a more stylish occasion, sharing an array of appetizers is a great way to reconnect with old friends and make some new ones!

Sharon's PARTY TIP

Sharing good food with family and friends in a relaxed setting and making them feel welcome – that is Sharon Dierberg's entertaining philosophy. She and her husband Bob, Chairman of Dierbergs Markets, enjoy hosting gatherings for all occasions. Look for Sharon's party tips throughout this book.

The *Eat Hearty* logo indicates recipes that meet heart-healthy criteria. For more information, see page 93.

The Art of the Party

Entertaining is about getting together with favorite people and making them feel welcome. Here are our suggestions for adding your personal style and making it all come together easily.

The Host

- Everyone will have a much better time if you – the host – isn't frazzled and exhausted. Remember the mighty cliché: *Less is more.*

- Keep the number of invitations manageable so you and the guests can really enjoy each other's company.

The Plan

- Forget themes and think mood – a warm summer evening on the patio; cozy wine and cheese by the fire; stylish Saturday night cocktails and appetizers; a casual Wednesday night get-together.

- Be clear on the invitations so guests know what to expect.

The Food

It's fun to create a signature appetizer – one that everyone anticipates when they are invited to your house. Choose a couple recipes that can be made-ahead and frozen. Supplement your menu with favorites from Dierbergs Deli, then review your menu plan, remembering the four "T's" – taste, texture, temperature, and trouble-free.

- **Taste** Serve an assortment of flavors to keep things interesting – something savory, sweet, mild, and spicy or assertive. Stick with fresh fruits and vegetables that are in season. It's better to have a few that taste great than a bunch that are just so-so.

- **Texture** Crisp veggies and crackers, flaky pastry-wrapped appetizers, chewy breads, juicy fruit, and creamy cheeses and dips make the menu more inviting.

- **Temperature** A few hot hors d'oeuvres and some chilled items will create a nice balance and be reasonable to serve at the right temperature. And you can't go wrong with anything that tastes best served at room temperature, like cheeses, olives, and nuts.

- **Trouble-Free** Rely on ready-to go-items like olives, nuts, skinny bread sticks, crostini, jars of marinated feta, pretzels, and gourmet mustards that are easy to keep on hand.

The Service

Cocktail parties are often a casual buffet of tasty appetizers, but you may want to walk around with trays of hors d'oeuvres to offer guests. Or why not do both! The party venue will help decide what works best.

- Spread food out among smaller tables placed throughout the room so guests will mingle.

- Vary the sizes, shapes, and heights of your serving pieces. A cake stand can be perfect for appetizers!

- Cruise by the buffet table occasionally and refill or refresh platters as needed.

- Re-purpose glass candle holders to serve peanuts, cashews, or candies.

- Don't forget the small stuff: small dishes for nut shells and olive pits; serving utensils and ice tongs; napkins and wooden picks.

- Add garnishes to the list – a fresh herb sprig, citrus slices, edible flowers, or a green onion fan. A little something extra will give your platters and trays a finished look.

Cocktail Party Math

Party in a Flash

Flash freeze a batch of your favorite appetizers and you can host a party at a moment's notice. This easy technique keeps appetizers separated so you can heat as many as you need.

Here's how:
Make appetizers according to recipe directions. Cook appetizers like meatballs, crab rangoon, or won tons as directed. Do not bake pastry-wrapped appetizers.

Place individual appetizers in a single layer on jellyroll pans and cover tightly.

Freeze 1 hour or until firm.

Transfer frozen appetizers to airtight containers or freezer-weight plastic bags.

Label containers with date, and original baking time and temperature. Store in the freezer up to 1 month.

Do not thaw unbaked appetizers before cooking. Bake them from the frozen state allowing 5 to 10 minutes additional time.

Thaw cooked appetizers in the refrigerator overnight. Bake them in a 425°F. oven just until heated through, about 10 minutes.

Hosting a cocktail party is cool; running out of something is not! Here are some guidelines to help you plan for your special occasion.

Appetizers

The length of the party affects the amount of food you'll need. For a 30-minute cocktail hour before dinner, plan on 4 to 6 hors d'oeuvres per person. If the party is 2 to 3 hours long, allow 10 to 12 appetizers per person.

Decide how many varieties of appetizers to serve based on the number of guests attending.

Number of Guests	Types of Appetizers	Number of Each/Person
8 to10	4	3 to 4
14 to 16	5 to 6	2 to 3
20 to 30	7 to 8	1 to 2

Cocktails and Libations

For a 1-hour party, plan for 2 beverages per guest. For a 2- to 3-hour party, plan on 1 beverage per person per hour. Basic tumblers and wine glasses (2 per person) are ideal for most parties.

Small bowls of lemon and lime wedges, half slices of oranges and cucumbers, olives and maraschino cherries make great drink garnishes.

Wine/champagne (750 ml)	Six 4-ounce glasses
Beer (1 case)	Twenty-four 12-ounce servings
Soda (2 liter)	Eleven 6-ounce glasses
Liquor (750 ml)	25.6 ounces
Punch (1 gallon)	Twenty 6-ounce servings
Coffee (1 pound)	Fifty 6-ounce cups
Ice cubes	1 pound/guest

Tiny Bubbles

A bit of bubbly Champagne or sparkling wine adds a special touch to any occasion. Here are some tips to keep the bubbles flowing.

- Champagne styles, listed dry to sweet: brut, extra dry/extra sec, sec, demi-sec.
- Serve in champagne flutes, not champagne saucers, to preserve the bubbles.
- To store a partial bottle of Champagne, insert the handle of a silver spoon in the neck of the bottle and chill. The silver creates a chemical reaction that maintains carbonation.

Dierbergs School of Cooking
Since 1978

Southroads Center
Tesson Ferry and I-270
St. Louis, MO 63128

West Oak Center
Olive Boulevard and
   Craig Road
Creve Coeur, MO 63141

Clarkson/Clayton Center
Clarkson and Clayton Roads
Ellisville, MO 63011

Bogey Hills Plaza
Zumbehl Road and I-70
St. Charles, MO 63303

Edwardsville Crossing
Troy Road and
   Governor's Parkway
Edwardsville, IL 62025

636-812-1336 (Missouri)
618-622-5353 (Illinois)

Explore the world of cooking at Dierbergs and have a little fun in our kitchen – and yours!

- Choose from dozens of topics from appetizers, entrées, or desserts to seafood, wines, restaurant specialties, regional cooking styles, ethnic foods, heart-healthy cooking, and much more.

- Classes taught by noted chefs, restaurateurs, cookbook authors, caterers, and staff instructors.

- Custom classes for birthday parties, special events, and corporate team-building.

For more information on Dierbergs School of Cooking or cooking class schedules:

www.dierbergs.com

cheese

Clockwise from upper left:
Pesto Sundried Tomato Torte, Point Reyes Original Blue Cheese,
Goat Cheese Rolled in Chopped Fresh Parsley, Chipotle Glazed
Pecans (recipe on page 77), Holland Gouda with Mediterranean
Herbs, Carr Valley Applewood Smoked Cheddar

Cheese and Wine Party Plan

If you want to get a party started, just say "cheese." The quintessential cheese tray is one of the simplest – and most popular – appetizers at any get-together. And you don't have to cook a thing!

It's impossible to list all of the wonderful cheeses from around the world. Mild and creamy, rich and robust – part of enjoying cheese is trying new varieties alongside your familiar favorites. Select a balance of flavors and textures for a well-rounded cheese tray, allowing one to two ounces per person. Start with a mild cheese, like fontina, havarti, or gouda. Add one with an edible rind, like brie, camembert, or muenster. Include a blue, maybe a stilton, or gorgonzola. And be sure to have a robust, full bodied choice like gruyère, cotija, feta, or aged provolone. To experience the flavor at its best, bring cheese to room temperature about 1 hour before serving.

Perfect Partners

Cheese plays very well with others. Serve plain breads and crackers so you can appreciate all of the subtle flavors of each cheese. But don't forget that opposites attract. Add complimentary or contrasting flavors to make your cheese tray more interesting. Fruits that pair nicely include apples, pears, grapes, fresh figs, melons, and dried fruits. Avoid acidic fruits, like citrus. It's fun to have a few extras, like seasoned nuts, chutney, sausages, mustards, and jams.

Great Combinations

Keep the presentation simple and you'll have a cheese tray that is as inviting as it is delicious. You can never go wrong with just cheese, grapes, French bread, and wine. Want something more creative? Try some of our suggestions to get you started.

Oh, So French! Beautiful Raspberry Brie (page 15), chèvre, roquefort, comte, boursin, grapes, sliced baguette, Sauvignon Blanc, Cabernet Sauvignon

Summer Picnic Camembert, bel paese, blue cheese, berries, melon, crusty white bread, water crackers, *Mini Lemon Cheesecakes (page 86),* Champagne, Pinot Noir

By The Fire Brie and Wild Mushroom Fondue (page 14), Manchego, port-salut, stilton, aged gouda, apples, dried apricots, Marcona almonds, whole grain bread, Chardonnay, Zinfandel

Watching The Game Reuben in Rye (page 71), jarlsberg, muenster, cheddar, havarti, apples, summer sausage, wheat crackers, chutney, stone ground mustard, Bock Beer, Riesling, Shiraz

A Little Bit Italian Mediterranean Feta Bites (page 59), mozzarella, gorgonzola, asiago, fresh figs, grapes, sun-dried tomatoes, salami, pine nuts, olives, focaccia, bread sticks, Pinot Grigio, Chianti

After Dinner Stilton, Saint André with fig spread, English cheddar, pears, glazed walnuts, *Chocolate Nut Fillo Pencils (page 89),* Gewürztraminer, Port

Cranberry Brie Mini Fillo Tarts

Sweet and tangy cranberry compote and creamy brie come together in crisp pastry shells for a festive appetizer that will have everyone talking.

1 cup fresh cranberries
1/3 cup sugar
1/4 cup water
1 pear, cored and finely diced
1/2 teaspoon almond extract
1 round (8 ounces) brie
  cheese
2 boxes (1.9 ounces each)
  frozen mini fillo shells
Sliced almonds, toasted

In medium saucepan, combine cranberries, sugar, and water; bring to a boil over medium-high heat. Reduce heat and cook stirring occasionally for 5 minutes. Stir in pear; cook stirring occasionally for 2 minutes. Stir in extract.

Using edge of teaspoon, scrape white rind from top and sides of brie; cut brie into 30 cubes. Place 1 cheese cube in each fillo cup; top with 1 teaspoon cranberry mixture. Place on baking sheet. Bake in 400°F. oven until cheese begins to melt, about 5 minutes. Arrange on serving platter; garnish each tart with almond slice.

Makes 30 Tarts

TIP Frozen mini fillo shells, located in the frozen food aisle, make this recipe easy, but when you have time, homemade shells are so fresh, flaky, and easy to make! See our recipe below.

Mini Fillo Shells

It takes just a few minutes to make a big batch of these crisp and delicate shells. Then fill them with just about anything sweet or savory to add an elegant touch to your party table.

8 ounces (1/2 of 16-ounce
  twin package) frozen fillo
  dough, thawed in
  refrigerator overnight
5 tablespoons butter, melted,
  or butter flavor no-stick
  cooking spray

Unroll fillo onto work surface. Cover completely with plastic wrap. Place 1 sheet fillo on clean dry surface; brush with butter or coat with cooking spray. Top with 4 fillo sheets, brushing each sheet with butter. Using sharp knife, cut into twelve 3-inch squares; discard excess fillo. Press each fillo square, buttered-side down, into mini muffin cup with corners extending above edges of pan. Repeat with remaining fillo and butter. Bake in 400°F. oven until crisp and golden brown, about 4 minutes. Store in airtight container at room temperature.

Makes 4 dozen

Brie and Wild Mushroom Fondue

This luxurious fondue, created by Dierbergs School of Cooking Manager Jennifer Kassel, is pure indulgence. A medley of sautéed mushrooms adds an earthy richness to the smooth, creamy cheese.

2 teaspoons olive oil
6 ounces wild mushrooms (baby bella, shiitake, oyster), stemmed and diced (about 2 cups)
2 tablespoons minced shallot
1/4 cup chopped fresh parsley
1 teaspoon fresh thyme leaves
2 rounds (8 ounces each) brie cheese
1 package (3 ounces) cream cheese, cut into cubes
2 tablespoons flour
1 cup dry white wine
Ground black pepper to taste
1 loaf (8 ounces) French baguette, cut into bite-size cubes

In medium skillet, heat olive oil over medium heat. Add mushrooms, shallot, parsley, and thyme; cook stirring occasionally until mushrooms soften, about 2 to 3 minutes. Remove from heat; set aside.

Using edge of teaspoon, scrape white rind from top and sides of brie; cut brie into cubes. In medium bowl, combine brie and cream cheese. Sprinkle flour over top; toss until well mixed.

In medium saucepan, bring wine to a simmer over medium heat. Add cheese cubes; cook stirring freqently until melted and smooth. Stir in mushroom mixture and season with pepper. Transfer to fondue pot. Serve immediately with bread cubes.

Makes about 3 cups (12 servings)

Sharon's
PARTY TIP

Fondue is a great hands-on appetizer and gets everyone to mingle. I like to keep it warm in a mini-slow cooker.

Beautiful Raspberry Brie

Simple and elegant, this appetizer from Sharon Dierberg's personal collection always gets rave reviews and many requests for the recipe. Be prepared to share it with your friends, too!

1 round (8 ounces) brie cheese
2 tablespoons butter (divided)
1 cup Trappist red raspberry jam (divided)
3 tablespoons sliced almonds
Dierbergs Bakery Toasted French Bread Slices (crostini), lahvosh, or Granny Smith apple slices

Using edge of teaspoon, scrape white rind from top and sides of brie. Place brie in 9-inch glass pie plate or shallow baking dish. Dot with 2 teaspoons of the butter. Spread 2 tablespoons jam over brie. Dot brie and pie plate with remaining butter. Sprinkle almonds over top. Spoon remaining jam over brie and pie plate.

Bake in 350°F. oven until jam starts to bubble and brie has softened, about 15 minutes. Remove from oven. Cover and let stand 5 minutes. Serve with crostini.

Makes 8 servings

Sharon's

PARTY TIP

This appetizer is festive, pretty, delicious, and absolutely easy! I usually serve it with Valley Lahvosh Hearts. Our friends and family love it, and I hope you enjoy it as well.

Per serving

Calories 243
Fat 12 g
Cholesterol 36 mg
Sodium 192 mg
Carbohydrate 28 g
Fiber 1 g

Baked Manchego Cheese

Spain's signature cheese, Manchego (mahn-CHAY-go), makes the perfect tapa, or small plate. Coat it with a savory nut crust and warm it until it's soft and creamy. Then serve on slices of Catalan Tomato Bread.

1 tablespoon olive oil
1/2 cup sliced almonds
1 teaspoon smoked paprika
   or Hungarian sweet paprika
1 teaspoon dried oregano,
   crushed
Dash ground cayenne pepper
1/3 cup panko bread crumbs
1/4 cup egg substitute, OR
   1 egg, beaten with
   1 tablespoon water
1 wedge (about 8 ounces)
   Manchego or sharp white
   cheddar cheese, at room
   temperature
Catalan Tomato Bread

In small skillet, heat olive oil over medium heat. Add almonds, paprika, oregano, and cayenne; cook stirring frequently until fragrant and toasted, about 3 to 4 minutes. Remove from heat; transfer to plate and cool to room temperature.

In shallow dish, combine almonds, panko, and egg substitute. Press mixture over cheese to adhere. Place on small foil-lined baking sheet.

Bake in 400°F. oven until cheese is slightly softened and crumbs are lightly toasted, about 10 minutes. Transfer cheese to serving platter. Serve warm with Catalan Tomato Bread.

Makes 8 servings

Catalan Tomato Bread

3 cloves garlic, peeled
1/2 teaspoon coarse salt
1/3 cup extra virgin olive oil
1 loaf (8 ounces) French
   baguette, cut into
   3/4-inch-thick slices
4 vine-ripened tomatoes,
   halved crosswise

Using sharp knife, mince garlic; sprinkle with salt while mashing to make paste. In small bowl, combine garlic paste with olive oil. Brush lightly over both sides of bread slices. Discard any remaining oil.

Working in batches, place bread slices on grid over medium-high heat; grill until lightly toasted and grill marks appear, about 1 to 2 minutes per side. Remove from grill; immediately rub one side of each bread slice with cut edge of tomato, allowing bread to absorb tomato pulp. Serve at room temperature, or warm briefly on grill before serving.

Makes about 2 dozen

Per 3 slices Calories 166; Fat 10 g; Cholesterol 0 mg; Sodium 284 mg; Carbohydrate 18 g; Fiber 1 g

**Per serving
with 3 slices Bread**

Calories 345
Fat 24 g
Cholesterol 30 mg
Sodium 478 mg
Carbohydrate 21 g
Fiber 2 g

Jezebel Cheese Log

Our interpretation of this Southern classic combines creamy cheese, sweet pineapple, and a kick of horseradish. It's a colorful addition to any appetizer menu.

1 package (8 ounces) cream cheese, softened
1 package (4 ounces) goat cheese, softened
4 ounces (1 cup) finely shredded sharp cheddar cheese
1/2 cup pineapple ice cream topping
1/2 cup chopped dried apricots
3 tablespoons diced red bell pepper
2 tablespoons prepared horseradish
1/2 teaspoon dry mustard
1 cup coarsely chopped pecans, toasted
Wheat crackers

In work bowl of food processor fitted with steel knife blade, process cream cheese, goat cheese, and cheddar cheese until smooth.

1 Shape into 8-inch-long log. **2** Wrap in plastic wrap; twist ends tightly. Chill at least 2 hours or up to 3 days.

In medium bowl, stir together pineapple topping, apricots, bell pepper, horseradish, and dry mustard until well mixed. Cover and chill for up to 3 days.

Just before serving, roll cheese log in toasted pecans, pressing to adhere. Spread sauce on serving plate; place cheese log on top. Serve with wheat crackers.

Makes 12-16 servings

Sharon's PARTY TIP

Cheese balls are always a big hit, but they can look "damaged" pretty quickly. I like to shape cheese logs, instead, so everyone can easily slice off a portion. The cheese remaining on the platter continues to look good throughout the rest of the party. Enjoy!

Per serving without crackers

Calories 178
Fat 14 g
Cholesterol 23 mg
Sodium 113 mg
Carbohydrate 11 g
Fiber 1 g

Goat Cheese with Tomato Basil Sauce

When it's her turn to host a dinner gathering, Laura Dierberg Padousis treats her friends to this chic yet simple first course. The combination of zesty tomatoes, fragrant basil, and tangy cheese is unbeatable.

1 cup tomato basil pasta
   sauce
1 log (10.5 ounces) goat
   cheese, cut into 16 slices
1 tablespoon extra virgin
   olive oil
Garlic pepper to taste
2 tablespoons thinly sliced
   fresh basil leaves
Dierbergs Bakery Toasted
   French Bread Slices
   (crostini)

Spread generous tablespoon pasta sauce in 8 shallow ramekins that have been lightly coated with no-stick cooking spray. Place 2 cheese slices slightly overlapping in each ramekin. Drizzle about 1/4 teaspoon olive oil over each cheese slice; season with garlic pepper. Bake in 350°F. oven until cheese is melted, about 12 minutes. Garnish with fresh basil. Serve warm with crostini.

Makes 8 servings

Sharon's

PARTY TIP

For a more casual party, my daughter Laura likes to layer everything in a 9-inch glass pie plate, bake it for about 15 minutes, and serve the crostini on the side.

ingredient savvy

Goat Cheese

The mildly tart flavor of goat cheese is a delightful change of pace. Also known as chèvre (SHEHV-ruh), it may be made entirely from goat's milk or in combination with cow's milk. Goat cheeses range from moist and creamy to dry and somewhat firm. Follow the *use by* date on the package, or keep no more than 2 weeks from date of purchase.

Per serving

Calories 137
Fat 10 g
Cholesterol 17 mg
Sodium 242 mg
Carbohydrate 5 g
Fiber 1 g

Muffuletta-Topped Cream Cheese

Let the good times roll! This zesty olive relish is as lively as Mardi Gras itself! It's a quick and colorful appetizer that you'll want to serve all year long.

1 jar (3 ounces) pimiento-stuffed green olives, drained and coarsely chopped
1 can (2.25 ounces) sliced ripe olives, drained
1 can (2.25 ounces) sliced kalamata olives, drained
1/4 cup finely chopped red onion
1 large clove garlic, minced
2 tablespoons olive oil
2 tablespoons fresh lemon juice
2 to 3 teaspoons prepared horseradish
1 to 2 teaspoons dried basil
1 package (8 ounces) cream cheese
Fresh basil sprig
Homemade Crostini (recipe on page 72)

In medium bowl, combine olives, onion, garlic, olive oil, lemon juice, horseradish, and dried basil. Cover and chill several hours or overnight to develop flavors.

Place cream cheese on serving plate; spoon olive mixture over top. Garnish with fresh basil sprig. Serve with Crostini.

Makes 6-8 servings

Sharon's
PARTY TIP

Keep a block of cream cheese plus a great topping on hand to equal an instant appetizer. My favorite is actually Stonewell Kitchens Roasted Garlic Onion Jam. Yum!

Per serving without Crostini

Calories 187
Fat 19 g
Cholesterol 30 mg
Sodium 460 mg
Carbohydrate 3 g
Fiber <1 g

Gorgonzola and Walnut Palmiers

Think stylish appetizers are hard to make? Think again! Palmiers (palm-YAYS) – crisp, flaky slices of puff pastry swirled with a sweet or savory filling – couldn't be more sophisticated or simple to prepare.

½ cup chopped walnuts
2 tablespoons diced shallot
1 teaspoon Italian herb
seasoning
1 package (8 ounces) cream
cheese, softened
4 ounces (1 cup) crumbled
gorgonzola cheese
1 box (17.3 ounces) frozen
puff pastry sheets, thawed
in refrigerator overnight
1 egg, beaten with
1 tablespoon water
Fresh herb sprigs

In work bowl of food processor fitted with steel knife blade, combine walnuts, shallot, and Italian seasoning; process until coarsely chopped. Add cream cheese and gorgonzola; pulse until well blended; set aside.

On lightly floured surface, roll one pastry sheet into 12 x 14-inch rectangle. Spread one-half of the cheese mixture on pastry leaving ½-inch border. **1** Beginning with long edge, roll pastry sheet from both sides to meet in center to resemble a scroll. Wrap in plastic wrap. Repeat with remaining pastry and filling. Chill at least 2 hours.

Remove plastic wrap. **2** Place pastry on cutting board; slice crosswise into ½-inch-thick slices. Place on parchment-lined baking sheets; brush tops lightly with egg mixture. Bake in 400°F. oven until pastry is golden brown and puffed, about 10 to 12 minutes. Arrange on serving platter; garnish with fresh herb sprigs. Serve warm or at room temperature.

Makes about 4 dozen

Sharon's

PARTY TIP

These taste best when they're freshly baked, so I slice and flash-freeze them unbaked (see Party in a Flash on page 8). Then I can bake just the number of appetizers I need from the frozen state so they're always hot and fresh. Lifesaver!

Zesty Beer Cheese Spread with Garlic Pretzels

Perfect for poker night, watching a football game, or just hanging out with friends, this hearty pub-style appetizer will be a hit – guaranteed!

1 package (8 ounces) shredded sharp cheddar cheese
1 loaf (8 ounces) pasteurized prepared cheese product (Velveeta), cubed
1/2 cup beer, at room temperature
2 tablespoons prepared horseradish
1/2 teaspoon dry mustard
4 to 5 drops hot pepper sauce

In work bowl of food processor fitted with steel knife blade, combine all ingredients; process until smooth, about 1 minute. Cover and chill several hours or overnight to develop flavors. Place in crock or serving bowl. Serve at room temperature with Garlic Pretzels.

Makes about 2 1/2 cups

Garlic Pretzels

1/4 cup butter
1 tablespoon honey
1/4 teaspoon garlic pepper
1 package (18 ounces) frozen soft pretzels

Place butter and honey in shallow microwave-safe dish. Microwave (high) for 45 seconds; stir in garlic pepper. Dip one side of each pretzel in butter mixture. Place buttered-side up on parchment-lined baking sheet. Sprinkle with salt (from package of pretzels). Bake according to package directions. Serve warm.

Makes 6 Pretzels

Per pretzel Calories 259; Fat 9 g; Cholesterol 20 mg; Sodium 953 mg; Carbohydrate 41 g; Fiber 1 g

Per 2 tablespoons Cheese

Calories 71
Fat 5 g
Cholesterol 17 mg
Sodium 232 mg
Carbohydrate 2 g
Fiber 0 g

seafood & meat

Fillo-Wrapped Shrimp
Recipe on page 28

Fillo-Wrapped Shrimp

When only something spectacular will do, these succulent shrimp are a must. And the Jack Daniel's Sauce is simply divine!

3 tablespoons fresh lemon juice
3 tablespoons Jack Daniel's whiskey
2 cloves garlic, minced
1/2 teaspoon lemon pepper seasoning
18 extra-large (16 to 20 count) shrimp, peeled and deveined leaving tails intact
6 thin slices prosciutto, each cut into 3 strips
8 ounces (1/2 of 16-ounce twin package) frozen fillo dough, thawed in refrigerator overnight
Butter flavor no-stick cooking spray
Jack Daniel's Sauce

Jack Daniel's Sauce

2 teaspoons olive oil
1/4 cup finely diced shallot
1 clove garlic, minced
1/2 cup Jack Daniel's whiskey
1 can (10.5 ounces) double strength beef broth
1 tablespoon teriyaki marinade
1 tablespoon cornstarch

In medium bowl, stir together lemon juice, whiskey, garlic, and lemon pepper. Add shrimp; gently toss until well mixed. Cover and chill for 1 hour.

Wrap one strip prosciutto around each shrimp; set aside.

Unroll 10 sheets fillo onto work surface. Cover completely with plastic wrap. (Refreeze remaining fillo package for another use.) Place 1 sheet fillo on clean dry surface; coat with cooking spray. Top with 4 fillo sheets, coating each sheet with cooking spray. Using sharp knife, cut lengthwise into 1-inch-wide strips. Starting with head end of shrimp, wrap one fillo strip around each shrimp in spiral fashion, covering entire shrimp except tail. Repeat with remaining fillo and shrimp. Place on parchment-lined baking sheet. Lightly coat wrapped shrimp with cooking spray. Bake in 400°F. oven until golden brown, about 10 to 12 minutes. Arrange on serving platter. Serve warm with Sauce.

Makes 1 1/2 dozen

In medium skillet, heat olive oil over medium-high heat. Add shallot and garlic; cook until shallot wilts, about 2 to 3 minutes. Add whiskey; cook until reduced by half, about 4 minutes. In small bowl, whisk together beef broth, marinade, and cornstarch; stir into shallot mixture. Cook stirring constantly until thickened, about 1 to 2 minutes. Strain if desired. Pour into serving bowl.

Makes about 1 1/4 cups

 Per 2 tablespoons Calories 50; Fat 1 g; Cholesterol 0 mg; Sodium 275 mg; Carbohydrate 3 g; Fiber 0 g

Per Shrimp with
1 tablespoon Sauce

Calories 95
Fat 3 g
Cholesterol 29 mg
Sodium 349 mg
Carbohydrate 9 g
Fiber <1 g

Dilled Shrimp

Ask Sharon Dierberg to name some of her family's favorite appetizers, and we'll bet that these succulent shrimp are at the top of the list. A generous sprinkle of dill adds a burst of flavor to the creamy sauce.

1 pound medium (43 to 50 count) frozen cooked shrimp
1¹/2 cups mayonnaise
¹/2 cup dairy sour cream
¹/3 cup fresh lemon juice
¹/4 cup sugar
2 tablespoons dried dill weed
¹/4 teaspoon salt
1 large red onion, thinly sliced (about 1¹/2 cups)
Lemon slices
Fresh dill sprigs

Completely thaw shrimp. If necessary, peel and devein shrimp; drain thoroughly.

In large bowl, stir together mayonnaise, sour cream, lemon juice, sugar, dill, and salt. Stir in shrimp and onion. Cover and chill for several hours or overnight.

Stir once; transfer shrimp to glass serving bowl. Place serving bowl in larger bowl of ice. Nestle slices of lemon and fresh dill sprigs among the ice.

Makes 8-10 servings

Sharon's

PARTY TIP

No matter how much you make, it's never enough! You'll want seafood or appetizer forks to serve this recipe. If you don't have a set, you can purchase party forks in Dierbergs Party Center.

Ice Bowls

Keeping chilled appetizers cool during a party is essential for food safety and makes whatever you're serving taste its very best. A large bowl made of ice adds drama to your table while it puts the chill on your appetizers.

You'll need two bowls of similar shape, one being a little smaller than the other. Fill the large bowl half-full with water. Set the smaller bowl inside the large bowl. Weight down the smaller bowl so the water remains underneath and surrounds the small bowl. Bags of frozen veggies work well as weights.

Freeze for at least 8 hours. When it's party time, place the ice bowl on a tray that's deep enough to catch drips and protect your table. Fill your ice bowl with chilled boiled shrimp, crab claws, or fresh fruit for the coolest party in town!

Per serving

Calories 312
Fat 27 g
Cholesterol 105 mg
Sodium 383 mg
Carbohydrate 8 g
Fiber <1 g

Martini Shrimp Cocktail

A crisp, dry martini meets the venerable shrimp starter for one cool and classy appetizer. The perfect garnish? Why olives, of course!

ingredient savvy

Shrimp

True, shrimp are higher in dietary cholesterol than most seafood, but they are very low in total and saturated fat. So shrimp *can* be part of a healthy eating plan.

Cooking shrimp in the shell gives the best flavor and texture. To devein shrimp in the shell, use kitchen shears to cut along the back edge of the shell. Remove the vein under cold running water.

Shrimp are sold by size, or count. Larger shrimp are more expensive but also more impressive and easier to clean.

Size	count/lb.
Jumbo	10-15
Extra-large	16-20
Large	26-30
Medium	43-50

Per serving

Calories 95
Fat 1 g
Cholesterol 78 mg
Sodium 410 mg
Carbohydrate 8 g
Fiber 1 g

1½ pounds large (26 to 30 count) shrimp
4 cups water
2 cups dry vermouth
1 lemon, thinly sliced
¼ teaspoon ground cayenne pepper
Martini Cocktail Sauce
Chopped green olives

Devein shrimp leaving shells intact (see sidebar). In large saucepan, bring water, vermouth, lemon slices, and cayenne pepper to a boil over medium-high heat. Add shrimp; return to a boil. Remove from heat, cover, and let stand until shrimp are opaque, about 2 to 3 minutes. Drain shrimp. Cover and chill for several hours. Remove shells leaving tails intact.

To serve, spoon Martini Cocktail Sauce into 8 martini glasses. Arrange shrimp around rim of glass. Garnish with chopped olives.

Makes 8 servings

Martini Cocktail Sauce

1 cup cocktail sauce
1 tablespoon fresh lemon juice
1 to 2 tablespoons gin or vodka

In small bowl, stir together all ingredients. Cover and chill for several hours to develop flavors.

Makes 1 cup

 Per 2 tablespoons Calories 35; Fat 0 g; Cholesterol 0 mg; Sodium 345 mg; Carbohydrate 8 g; Fiber 1 g

Sharon's

I love this take on shrimp cocktail! It's great as a first course before dinner. Or instead of just setting them on a buffet table, you can walk around with a tray of these "martinis" and greet your guests. Elegant and fun!

PARTY TIP

Mini Crab Cakes

These marvelous minis are a small plate favorite. Serve with an assortment of savory sauces to please everyone in your crowd.

1 egg, lightly beaten
1/4 cup mayonnaise
1/4 cup finely chopped onion
1/4 cup finely chopped red bell pepper
1 tablespoon minced fresh parsley
1 tablespoon fresh lemon juice
2 teaspoons Old Bay seasoning
2 cans (6.5 ounces each) white crab meat, drained and flaked
1/2 cup panko bread crumbs
Minced fresh parsley and red bell pepper
Dipping sauce (see TIP)

In large bowl, combine egg, mayonnaise, onion, bell pepper, parsley, lemon juice, and seasoning. Add crab meat and panko. Stir until evenly moistened; let stand 10 minutes. Shape crab mixture into 12 to 16 mini cakes.

Place on parchment-lined baking sheet. Bake in 425°F. oven until golden brown, about 10 minutes per side. Place on serving platter; garnish with confetti of parsley and red bell pepper. Serve with dipping sauce.

Makes 12-16 Mini Crab Cakes

TIP These crab cakes are great served with Horseradish Aïoli (recipe on page 35), Chipotle Aïoli (recipe on page 58), or Mango Salsa (recipe on page 42).

Sharon's

PARTY TIP

Bob and I sample crab cakes wherever we go, and these are delicious. Bob likes that they're baked, and I love the fact that there is no messy frying! Try them with all of the different dipping sauces. Enjoy!

Per 2 Crab Cakes

Calories 111
Fat 6 g
Cholesterol 84 mg
Sodium 522 mg
Carbohydrate 4 g
Fiber <1 g

Seafood Canapés

Simple and sophisticated, these elegant bites are perfect for a cocktail party, bridal shower, or other very special occasion. Garnish the tray with a confetti of snipped fresh parsley or chives.

2 boxes (1.9 ounces each) frozen mini fillo shells
Lobster Filling or Smoked Salmon Filling
Lemon slices, snipped fresh parsley, and snipped fresh chives for garnish

Bake fillo shells according to package directions. Place cooled shells back into plastic tray. Spoon Lobster Filling or pipe Smoked Salmon Filling into shells. Arrange on serving platter; garnish with lemon slices, parsley, and chives.

Makes 2½ dozen

Lobster Filling

1 small lemon, sliced
4 frozen slipper lobster tails (about 1 pound), thawed
½ cup dry vermouth
½ cup mayonnaise
1 shallot, finely diced
1 tablespoon chopped fresh parsley
¼ teaspoon ground white pepper
⅛ teaspoon salt

Place lemon slices in medium saucepan. Add lobster tails and vermouth; bring to a boil over medium-high heat. Reduce heat, cover, and simmer for 3 minutes. Turn off heat; let stand 5 minutes. Remove lobster; discard lemon slices and reserve vermouth mixture. Remove lobster meat from shells. Chop lobster meat; place in medium bowl.

In small bowl, whisk mayonnaise with 1 tablespoon of the reserved vermouth mixture until well blended. Stir in shallot, parsley, white pepper, and salt. Stir into lobster. Cover and chill up to 24 hours.

Smoked Salmon Filling

1 cup heavy whipping cream
1 package (5.2 ounces) Boursin garlic and herbs cheese
1 package (4.5 ounces) smoked salmon

In large chilled mixer bowl, beat whipping cream and Boursin at low speed until well combined. Beat at high speed until stiff peaks form, about 2 to 3 minutes. Remove and discard skin from salmon; finely flake with fork. Gently fold flaked salmon into cheese mixture. Place in large freezer-weight reclosable plastic bag; snip off one corner to make hole. Pipe into shells.

Per 2 Lobster Canapés

Calories 103
Fat 8 g
Cholesterol 7 mg
Sodium 117 mg
Carbohydrate 5 g
Fiber 0 g

Per 2 Smoked Salmon Canapés

Calories 149
Fat 13 g
Cholesterol 35 mg
Sodium 172 mg
Carbohydrate 5 g
Fiber 0 g

Tenderloin Napoleons with Horseradish Aïoli

The classic combination of beef tenderloin and horseradish gets dressed up for the cocktail hour. Crisp puff pastry adds a little flair to these bite-size sandwiches.

Puff Pastry

1 sheet (½ of 17.3-ounce box) frozen puff pastry, thawed in refrigerator overnight
1 egg, beaten with 1 tablespoon water
¾ to 1 pound beef tenderloin
2 tablespoons Dijon mustard
2 teaspoons herbes de Provence
1 teaspoon cracked black pepper
1 clove garlic, minced
Horseradish Aïoli
Fresh Italian parsley sprigs

On lightly floured surface, roll pastry sheet into 10 x 12-inch rectangle. Cut pastry lengthwise into 4 strips and crosswise into 3 strips, forming 12 rectangles. Place on parchment-lined baking sheet; brush with egg mixture. Bake in 400°F. oven until golden brown and puffed, about 12 to 15 minutes. Cool completely. Split each pastry in half to form a top and bottom; set aside.

Trim and discard fat from tenderloin. In small bowl, stir together mustard, herbes de Provence, pepper, and garlic; rub over tenderloin. Let stand at room temperature for 10 minutes. Place on rack in shallow roasting pan. Roast in 425°F. oven until internal temperature is 135°F. for medium-rare, about 35 to 40 minutes. Cover and let stand 15 minutes before thinly slicing.

Arrange pastry bottoms on serving platter. Top each with dollop of Aïoli, tenderloin slices, and pastry top. Garnish platter with fresh parsley sprigs.

Makes 1 dozen

TIP Beef petite shoulder tender can be substituted for the beef tenderloin. Roast according to directions for 25 minutes.

Frozen puff pastry equals easy elegance in a box! For best results, thaw pastry in the refrigerator overnight. For crisp pastry, bake it at a high temperature on a parchment-lined baking sheet. Add color and shine to the pastry by brushing it with a mixture of 1 egg beaten with 1 tablespoon water before baking. Use the egg mixture to seal edges and to attach pastry cut-outs to the top for a decorative touch.

Horseradish Aïoli

1 cup mayonnaise
2 tablespoons prepared horseradish
2 cloves garlic, minced
1 tablespoon minced fresh Italian parsley
Dash ground white pepper

In small bowl, combine all ingredients. Cover and chill several hours or overnight to develop flavors.

Makes 1 cup

Per 2 tablespoons Calories 183; Fat 20 g; Cholesterol 10 mg; Sodium 192 mg; Carbohydrate 1 g; Fiber <1 g

Per Napoleon

Calories 277
Fat 24 g
Cholesterol 42 mg
Sodium 302 mg
Carbohydrate 7 g
Fiber <1 g

Mediterranean Meatballs with Cucumber Aïoli

Dierbergs School of Cooking Manager Nancy Lorenz gives cocktail meatballs a delicious make-over. Stuffed with Greek olives and served with a garlicky dipping sauce, these will be a winner at your next gathering.

1/2 pound lean ground pork
1/2 pound lean ground beef
1 egg, lightly beaten
1/4 cup Italian seasoned
   bread crumbs
2 large cloves garlic, minced
1/2 teaspoon ground
   coriander
1/2 teaspoon salt
1/4 teaspoon ground black
   pepper
24 pitted kalamata olives,
   patted dry
Cucumber Aïoli
Lemon slices

In large bowl, combine all ingredients except olives, Aïoli, and lemon slices. Divide mixture into 24 equal portions. Enclose 1 olive in each portion of meat, forming into balls; place on foil-lined jellyroll pan. Bake in 350°F. oven until lightly browned, about 10 to 15 minutes. Place small bowl of Aïoli on serving platter; arrange Meatballs on platter and garnish with lemon slices.

Makes 2 dozen

Cucumber Aïoli

2 large cloves garlic, peeled
3/4 cup mayonnaise
1 large pickling cucumber,
   peeled, seeded, and diced
1/4 cup chopped red onion
1 tablespoon lemon juice
1 teaspoon dried dill weed

Fit food processor with steel knife blade. With machine running, drop garlic through feed tube; process until finely chopped. Add remaining ingredients; process until smooth. Place in serving bowl; cover and chill several hours or overnight to develop flavors.

Makes 1 1/4 cups

TIP If desired, baby cucumbers can be used in place of pickling cucumbers. There's no need to peel or seed, just dice and enjoy them.

Per 2 tablespoons Calories 114; Fat 12 g; Cholesterol 6 mg; Sodium 109 mg; Carbohydrate 1 g; Fiber <1 g

Italian Beef Spiedini

Make minis of this popular restaurant entrée for a terrific make-ahead appetizer. A swirl of lemon and garlic makes them irresistible.

2/3 cup Italian seasoned
   bread crumbs
1/3 cup grated parmesan
   cheese
1 tablespoon chopped fresh
   Italian parsley
2 teaspoons grated lemon
   peel
2 cloves garlic, minced
2 tablespoons butter
2 tablespoons olive oil
1 pound beef breakfast
   steaks (thinly sliced top
   round)
Wooden skewers, soaked in
   water for 30 minutes
Lemon slices
Fresh Italian parsley sprigs

On sheet of waxed paper, combine bread crumbs, cheese, parsley, lemon peel, and garlic. Place butter in glass pie plate. Microwave (high) for 30 seconds or until melted; stir in olive oil. Dip beef into butter mixture; coat both sides with crumb mixture. Tightly roll up beef; slice each roll into 1/2-inch-thick spirals. Thread 2 spirals onto each skewer. Dip cut sides into crumbs. Grill or broil as directed. Place Spiedini on serving platter; garnish with lemon slices and fresh parsley sprigs.

Makes 1 dozen

TO GRILL Place skewers on oiled grid over medium-high heat; cover and grill until cooked through and coating is lightly browned, about 3 to 4 minutes per side.

TO BROIL Place skewers on rack of broiler pan that has been lightly coated with no-stick cooking spray. Broil 6 inches from heat source until cooked through and browned, about 4 to 5 minutes per side.

Sharon's
PARTY TIP

I'm always on the lookout for appetizers that I can make ahead. You can assemble these Spiedini and freeze them for up to 1 week, then broil them from the frozen state for about 4 minutes per side. I wrap the ends of the skewers in foil so they don't char. Fun and different!

ingredient savvy

Breakfast Steak

Like many cuts of meat, Breakfast Steaks can have a different name depending on where you live. Finding what you want can be like reading aliases on a *Most Wanted* poster!

Breakfast Steaks – a.k.a. Sandwich Steaks or Minute Steaks – are cut from the round tip of the leg area. They are usually cut 1/8- to 1/4-inch thick, making them perfect for quick-cooking recipes.

Per skewer

Calories 109
Fat 6 g
Cholesterol 22 mg
Sodium 209 mg
Carbohydrate 5 g
Fiber <1 g

Pork Bruschetta with Orange Chimichurri

Spoon this famous Argentinean herb sauce over mini open-faced pork tenderloin sandwiches for a lively appetizer.

cuisine savvy

Chimichurri

In Argentina, where beef is king, no table is complete without chimichurri sauce. This lively blend of olive oil, vinegar, garlic, parsley, and herbs is the go-to sauce for spooning over slices of tender, juicy steak, hot off the grill.

As the old saying goes, *imitation is the sincerest form of flattery*, and we know a good thing when we taste it. We added a splash of orange juice and a sprinkle of freshly grated orange peel to our version of this venerable sauce. It's a great finishing touch for crispy toasts topped with slices of savory roasted pork tenderloin.

1 pork tenderloin
   (about 1 pound)
2 tablespoons Dijon mustard
2 large cloves garlic, minced
2 teaspoons grated lemon
   peel
1/2 teaspoon coarse salt
1/2 teaspoon ground cumin
1/2 teaspoon Hungarian
   sweet paprika
1/4 teaspoon crushed red
   pepper flakes
Homemade Crostini
   (recipe on page 72)
Orange Chimichurri
Fresh cilantro sprigs
Orange slices

Orange Chimichurri

1 large clove garlic, peeled
1/2 cup fresh cilantro leaves
1/2 cup fresh basil leaves
2 tablespoons grated orange
   peel
3 tablespoons fresh orange
   juice
1/2 teaspoon ground cumin
1/4 teaspoon salt
1/4 teaspoon ground black
   pepper
3 tablespoons olive oil

Trim and discard fat and silver skin from tenderloin. In small bowl, combine mustard, garlic, lemon peel, salt, cumin, paprika, and red pepper flakes. Rub over all sides of pork. Place pork on rack in shallow roasting pan. Roast in 400°F. oven until internal temperature is 155°F., about 20 to 25 minutes. Cover and let stand 10 minutes before thinly slicing on the diagonal.

Arrange Crostini on serving platter or tray; top each with pork slices and 1 teaspoon Orange Chimichurri. Garnish with fresh cilantro sprigs and orange slices.

Makes 18-20 appetizers

Fit food processor with steel knife blade. With machine running, drop garlic through feed tube; process until finely chopped. Add cilantro, basil, orange peel and juice, cumin, salt, and pepper; process until puréed. With machine running, pour olive oil through feed tube in slow, steady stream; process until well combined. Store in refrigerator up to 24 hours.

Makes about 1/2 cup

Per 2 tablespoons Calories 102; Fat 10 g; Cholesterol 0 mg; Sodium 147 mg; Carbohydrate 3 g; Fiber 1 g

Per appetizer

Calories 77
Fat 3 g
Cholesterol 14 mg
Sodium 189 mg
Carbohydrate 7 g
Fiber <1 g

Pot Stickers with Chili Garlic Sauce

Cathy Chipley, co-host of Dierbergs Presents Everybody Cooks® TV show, likes to cook these little bundles so they caramelize and stick to the pot, then steam them until they're done. Your guests will devour these tasty little bundles as fast as you can make them!

1 pound lean ground pork
2/3 cup angel hair cole slaw
1/2 cup minced red bell pepper
1/4 cup finely chopped green onion
2 tablespoons snipped fresh cilantro
2 cloves garlic, minced
2 teaspoons minced fresh ginger root
1 1/2 tablespoons soy sauce
1 teaspoon dark sesame oil
1 egg, lightly beaten
Salt and pepper to taste
1 package (16 ounces) won ton wrappers
2 tablespoons vegetable oil (divided)
Fresh cilantro sprigs
Chili Garlic Sauce

Chili Garlic Sauce

1 cup sugar
1/2 cup white rice vinegar
1/2 teaspoon salt
3 tablespoons chopped roasted peanuts (optional)
3 tablespoons snipped fresh cilantro
1 tablespoon chili purée with garlic

In large bowl, stir together ground pork, slaw, bell pepper, green onion, cilantro, garlic, ginger, soy sauce, sesame oil, egg, salt, and pepper. Place generous teaspoon pork mixture in center of 1 wrapper. Moisten edges of wrapper with water; gather 4 corners of wrapper together in center and pinch to seal. Repeat with remaining wrappers and filling.

In large nonstick skillet, heat 1 tablespoon of the oil over medium heat. Place half of the pot stickers flat-sides down in skillet; cook until bottoms are golden brown, about 3 minutes. Add 1/2 cup water; cover and steam over medium heat until tender, about 3 to 4 minutes. Arrange on serving platter; cover and keep warm. Repeat procedure with remaining pot stickers. Garnish with fresh cilantro sprigs. Serve warm with Chili Garlic Sauce.

Makes about 4 dozen

In small saucepan, combine sugar, vinegar, and salt; bring to a boil over medium-high heat stirring frequently. Reduce heat and simmer stirring frequently until slightly thickened, about 5 to 7 minutes. Remove from heat; stir in peanuts, cilantro, and chili purée. Serve warm or at room temperature.

Makes 1 1/4 cups

Per 2 tablespoons Calories 84; Fat 0 g; Cholesterol 0 mg; Sodium 177 mg; Carbohydrate 21 g; Fiber 0 g

Tandoori Chicken Bites

Chicken flavored with the fragrant Indian spice blend, garam masala (gah-RAHM mah-SAH-lah), tops squares of flaky puff pastry for a savory appetizer that is sure to be a hit with your guests.

Garam Masala

1/2 pound boneless, skinless chicken breast halves, lightly pounded to even thickness
3/4 teaspoon garam masala (divided)
1 tablespoon vegetable oil
1 package (8 ounces) cream cheese, softened
4 ounces (1 cup) shredded monterey jack cheese
1/4 cup Major Grey's chutney
1/4 cup thinly sliced green onion (green portion only)
1 box (17.3 ounces) frozen puff pastry sheets, thawed in refrigerator overnight
1 egg, beaten with 1 tablespoon water
Chopped fresh cilantro or parsley

Season chicken with 1/2 teaspoon of the garam masala. In medium skillet, heat oil over medium-high heat. Add chicken; cook until internal temperatue is 165°F., about 3 to 4 minutes per side. Cool completely before dicing.

In medium bowl, combine cooked chicken, cream cheese, monterey jack cheese, chutney, green onion, and remaining 1/4 teaspoon garam masala.

On lightly floured surface, roll one pastry sheet into 12-inch square. Cut into thirty-six 2-inch squares. Brush with egg mixture; place on parchment-lined baking sheets. Repeat with remaining pastry. Place 1 teaspoon chicken filling in center of each square. Bake in 400°F. oven until pastry is golden brown and puffed, about 12 to 14 minutes. Arrange on serving platter; sprinkle cilantro over tops.

Makes 6 dozen

Garam masla is a warm and wonderful spice blend that is a staple of Indian cooking. The exact list of spices can vary, but one whiff will tell you that this combination of cinnamon, black pepper, cardamom, cloves, cumin, and nutmeg is a *must-have* for any well-stocked pantry. Look for garam masala in the spice section.

Combine 1 teaspoon or more of garam masala with 1 tablespoon each of brown sugar and coarse salt, and rub over chicken or pork before roasting for a rich flavor. Brush salmon fillets with maple syrup and sprinkle on the spice blend before grilling for a simple and spectacular entrée. Spritz pita bread triangles with no-stick cooking spray, dust with garam masala, then bake for crispy chips to serve with hummus.

Sharon's
PARTY TIP

These little pastries have great flavor and are a nice change of pace for a party menu. And you can assemble them ahead, flash-freeze them (see Party in a Flash on page 8), and bake them just before serving. Deliciously different!

Per 2 appetizers

Calories 106
Fat 7 g
Cholesterol 18 mg
Sodium 124 mg
Carbohydrate 6 g
Fiber 0 g

Chicken Quesadillas with Mango Salsa

Get ready for a fiesta! Tender chicken, zesty black beans, and a jalapeño-spiked Mango Salsa make these hearty quesadillas a great party-starter.

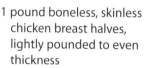

1 pound boneless, skinless
    chicken breast halves,
    lightly pounded to even
    thickness
2 teaspoons chili powder
1 tablespoon olive oil
1/2 cup finely chopped onion
3 cloves garlic, minced
1 can (15 ounces) black
    beans, rinsed and drained
1/2 cup chicken broth
1 teaspoon ground cumin
8 flour tortillas
    (8-inch diameter)
4 ounces (1 cup) shredded
    monterey jack cheese
Mango Salsa

Season chicken with chili powder. In large skillet, heat olive oil over medium-high heat. Add chicken; cook until internal temperature is 165°F., about 3 to 4 minutes per side. Let chicken stand 5 minutes before dicing.

In same skillet over medium-high heat, cook onion and garlic stirring frequently until onions wilt. Add beans, broth, and cumin; cook stirring frequently until heated through. Using potato masher or fork, mash beans to form thick paste. Spread bean mixture over half of each tortilla; top with chicken and cheese. Fold each tortilla in half.

Place quesadillas, one at a time, in large nonstick skillet over medium-high heat; cook until cheese is melted and tortillas are crisp, about 2 minutes per side. Cut each quesadilla into 3 wedges. Place on serving platter; serve with Salsa.

Makes 2 dozen

Mango Salsa

1 mango
1/2 cup finely diced red bell
    pepper
1/4 cup finely diced red onion
1 jalapeño, halved, seeded,
    deveined, and finely diced
2 tablespoons snipped fresh
    cilantro or parsley
1 teaspoon grated lime peel
2 tablespoons fresh lime
    juice
1 tablespoon olive oil
1 teaspoon honey

Hold mango stem-end up on cutting board. Make vertical slice along one of the long sides, about 3/8 inch from stem, following curve of seed. Make second slice on other side, about 3/8 inch from stem. (The long seed will be in center slice.) **1** Place double layer of clean kitchen towel in your hand. Hold one of the slices in your hand. Using tip of sharp knife, score mango into 3/4-inch cubes, being careful not to cut through peel. Push up on center to turn mango inside-out. **2** Run knife just above mango skin to slice away cubes. Repeat procedure with other mango half. Cut remaining mango away from seed and peel; cut into cubes. In medium bowl, combine diced mango and remaining ingredients; stir to combine. Cover and chill 2 hours to develop flavors.

Makes about 2 1/2 cups

Per 2 tablespoons Calories 16; Fat 1 g; Cholesterol 0 mg;
Sodium 1 mg; Carbohydrate 3 g; Fiber <1 g

Per 2 wedges without Salsa

Calories 208
Fat 7 g
Cholesterol 23 mg
Sodium 337 mg
Carbohydrate 24 g
Fiber 4 g

Greek Chicken Kabobs

Keep this recipe handy. Chicken tenders coated in savory Greek spices and served with a cool, creamy dipping sauce might just be the quickest and tastiest appetizer on the planet!

ingredient savvy

Avocados

Avocados are ripe when they yield to gentle pressure. To make sure they're ready when you are, buy them a day or two before you plan to use them.

Avocados darken quickly, so cut them just before serving. To remove the large pit in the center, cut lengthwise around the pit and gently twist the halves apart. Crumple a clean kitchen towel, place it on a cutting board, and nestle the avocado half with the pit in it. Strike the pit with a sharp knife and twist the knife to remove the pit.

Carefully scoop the flesh out of the skin with a spoon and slice or dice the avocado to use in salads, sandwiches, or guacamole.

1 pound chicken tenders
1 teaspoon dried oregano
1/2 teaspoon ground coriander
1/2 teaspoon salt
1/2 teaspoon ground black pepper
1/4 teaspoon garlic powder
1/4 teaspoon onion powder
Wooden skewers, soaked in water for 30 minutes
Fresh oregano sprigs
Lemon slices
Avocado Yogurt Sauce

If desired, remove tendons from chicken. Grasp tendon with paper towel. Use kitchen shears to scrape meat away from tendon. Place chicken in large reclosable plastic bag. In small bowl, combine oregano, coriander, salt, pepper, garlic powder, and onion powder. Sprinkle over chicken; seal bag and shake to coat chicken. Weave 1 chicken tender onto each skewer. Grill or broil as directed. Arrange kabobs on serving platter; garnish with fresh oregano and lemon slices. Serve with Avocado Yogurt Sauce.

Makes about 10 Kabobs

TO GRILL Place skewers on oiled grid over medium-high heat; cover and grill until cooked through and browned, about 4 to 5 minutes per side.

TO BROIL Place skewers on rack of broiler pan that has been lightly coated with no-stick cooking spray. Broil 6 inches from heat source until cooked through and browned, about 4 to 5 minutes per side.

Avocado Yogurt Sauce

2 cloves garlic, peeled
1 avocado, halved, seeded, peeled, and diced
1 carton (6 ounces) low-fat plain yogurt
2 teaspoons fresh lemon juice
3/4 teaspoon salt
1/4 teaspoon ground black pepper

Fit food processor with steel knife blade. With machine running, drop garlic through feed tube; process until finely chopped. Add remaining ingredients; process until smooth. Place in serving bowl; cover and chill several hours or overnight to develop flavors.

Makes 1 1/2 cups

 Per 2 tablespoons Calories 28; Fat 2 g; Cholesterol 1 mg; Sodium 156 mg; Carbohydrate 2 g; Fiber 1 g

Per Kabob without Sauce

Calories 33
Fat <1 g
Cholesterol 17 mg
Sodium 132 mg
Carbohydrate <1 g
Fiber <1 g

Devil's Own Hot Wing

A pile of sticky, spicy, and delightfully messy wings never fails to attract a crowd. Serve these with plenty of napkins.

3 pounds frozen chicken wing portions or drummettes
3 tablespoons Old Bay seasoning
1/2 teaspoon ground cayenne pepper
1/2 cup Dijon mustard
1/4 cup honey
3 tablespoons butter
2 tablespoons hot pepper sauce
2 tablespoons lemon juice
2 teaspoons Worcestershire sauce
2 cloves garlic, minced

Place frozen wings in large reclosable plastic bag. In small bowl, combine Old Bay and cayenne pepper; reserve 2 teaspoons. Add remaining seasoning to wings. Seal bag; shake to coat wings.

Place frozen wings in single layer on rack of broiler pan that has been lightly coated with no-stick cooking spray. Bake in 400°F. oven for 25 minutes. Turn wings and bake until lightly browned and thoroughly cooked, about 20 minutes.

Combine reserved seasoning with remaining ingredients in 2-cup glass measure. Microwave (high) stirring once for 2 minutes or until butter is melted and sauce is smooth.

Place wings in large serving bowl. Drizzle sauce over; toss to coat.

Makes about 2 1/2 dozen

TIP Heat levels vary for hot sauces. We used Tabasco hot pepper sauce in this recipe.

Sharon's PARTY TIP

Spicy chicken wings are always a hit at our house. I like to cook them and then put them in an electric skillet on low heat so they stay hot throughout the party. These are very spicy, so you might want to start with a little hot sauce and then add more to taste.

cuisine savvy

Chicken Wings

Once upon a time, chicken wings were of little use to anyone – except perhaps the chicken. They were just spare parts saved only for the sake of making soup.

But in 1964, faced with a bunch of hungry friends, restaurateur Teressa Bellissimo created what is now perhaps the most popular appetizer of all time – Buffalo Chicken Wings. The Anchor Bar in Buffalo, New York, was where Teressa fried that first batch of wings, dipped them in spicy sauce, and served them up in the wee hours with a pile of celery sticks and blue cheese dressing. The rest is history!

Whether you are a purist or the adventurous type, a pile of zesty chicken wings is guaranteed to have everyone flocking to your table!

Per 2 Wings

Calories 200
Fat 14 g
Cholesterol 90 mg
Sodium 818 mg
Carbohydrate 5 g
Fiber <1 g

veggies & fruit

Crisp Vegetable Dippers
See page 48

Crisp Vegetable Dippers

If your usual repertoire seldom ventures beyond a pile of baby carrots and a fistful of celery sticks, it's time to transform it into a creative crudités display. Think outside the bushel basket and mix it up a little. Cut new shapes, lightly blanch heartier veggies, or group items by color or theme. Even the simplest of dips will taste fresh, new, and exciting!

A Cut Above

- Cut large carrots into ¼-inch-thick bias slices to make oval shaped carrot chips. Bonus – they hold more dip!

- Slice cauliflower and large mushrooms into ¼-inch-thick slices for a new look.

- Dress up your display with a few green onion fans. Trim off root ends and cut the green portion of the onion into narrow strips, leaving the bulb of the onion intact. Place in a bowl of ice water for at least 30 minutes (or chill for several hours) until the ends curl. Try it with celery sticks, too.

Serve Something Unexpected

- Blanch heartier vegetables like asparagus, green beans, and sugar snap peas and add them to your lineup for new flavors, colors, and textures.

- Cut heads of radicchio into wedges and trim away the core, or split heads of Belgian endive in half. Rinse and separate the leaves and dry thoroughly. Voila! Instant vegetable scoops!

Show Off a New Look

- Channel your inner designer and let the shape of your serving tray inspire you. Arrange veggies in rows, rings, wedges – whatever catches your eye.

- Tumble crudités in a large shallow basket for a fresh, colorful look.

- Stand spears of your favorite veggies in glass tumblers. Group tumblers on a tray or just arrange on the table.

- Go green! Asparagus, green beans, sugar snap peas, cucumber, and zucchini spears look cool and inviting. Or think bold and bright! Carrot chips, red and yellow bell pepper strips, yellow summer squash spears, whole radishes, and radicchio wedges will be a colorful standout.

---

technique savvy

Blanching

There are some vegetables that you probably wouldn't serve raw, but that doesn't mean they wouldn't be a great addition to your next vegetable tray. Blanching – a quick dip in hot water – takes the edge off of sturdy vegetables and leaves just enough crunch behind.

To blanch, bring a medium pot of water to a boil over high heat. Add vegetables (about 1 cup at a time) and cook for 1 to 2 minutes.

Use a slotted spoon to transfer the veggies to a bowl of ice water to stop the cooking. Drain them on paper towels and chill until you're ready to dip.

Cremini Crostini

A blend of creamy cheeses and a medley of sautéed mushrooms tops crisp little toasts for a simply delicious appetizer.

2 tablespoons butter
1/2 pound wild mushrooms, sliced (cremini, baby bella, oyster, shiitake, button, or a combination)
1/4 cup drained and chopped sun-dried tomatoes in oil
2 tablespoons snipped fresh chives
1/4 teaspoon crushed red pepper flakes
1 package (8 ounces) cream cheese, cut into cubes
2 ounces (1/2 cup) crumbled blue cheese
Homemade Crostini (recipe on page 72)
Snipped fresh chives

In medium skillet, melt butter over medium-high heat. Add mushrooms, sun-dried tomatoes, the 2 tablespoons chives, and red pepper flakes; cover and cook stirring occasionally until mushrooms soften, about 5 minutes. Add cream cheese and blue cheese; cook stirring constantly until melted, about 2 minutes. Remove from heat; cool to room temperature.

Place Crostini on parchment-lined baking sheet; top each with 1 tablespoon mushroom mixture. Bake in 375°F. oven until topping is hot and bubbly, about 5 minutes. Place on serving platter; garnish with chives.

Makes 2-3 dozen

Sharon's

PARTY TIP

If you're tight on time, serve the mushroom mixture as a dip in a chafing dish or mini-slow cooker with the crostini in a basket alongside. You can make the mushroom mixture one to two days ahead and warm it just before serving.

ingredient savvy
Wild Mushrooms

Wild mushrooms add interesting flavor and texture to recipes. Remove tough stems from shiitake and portabella mushrooms. They are great to flavor soups, stocks, or sauces.

The gills from the underside of portabella caps cause some recipes to turn dark. Remove them before using by gently scraping with a spoon.

Mushrooms absorb water like a sponge and quickly become mushy. Store mushrooms in a paper bag or loosely covered in the refrigerator to extend their life. To clean them, simply wipe them with a damp paper towel.

Per Crostini

Calories 63
Fat 4 g
Cholesterol 10 mg
Sodium 97 mg
Carbohydrate 6 g
Fiber <1 g

Prosciutto and Chèvre-Stuffed Mushrooms

Just a few well-chosen ingredients make this cocktail party classic something truly special. Recipe from Dierbergs School of Cooking Instructor and St. Louis Post-Dispatch Food Columnist Mary Billings.

30 large button mushrooms
  (1½-inch diameter)
4 tablespoons butter, melted
2 tablespoons olive oil
½ cup chopped pecans,
  toasted
½ cup Italian seasoned bread
  crumbs
¼ cup diced prosciutto
1 package (5.3 ounces) goat
  cheese, softened
Additional Italian seasoned
  bread crumbs
Fresh herb sprigs

Rinse mushrooms and pat dry; remove and discard stems. Place mushrooms in large reclosable plastic bag; add butter and olive oil. Seal bag; shake to coat.

In medium bowl, stir together pecans, bread crumbs, and prosciutto. Add cheese; stir until well mixed. Spoon mixture into mushroom caps. Place mushrooms on parchment-lined jellyroll pan; drizzle any remaining butter mixture over mushrooms. Sprinkle mushroom tops with additional bread crumbs. Bake in 375°F. oven until heated through, about 10 minutes. Place on serving platter; garnish with fresh herb sprigs.

Makes 2½ dozen

MAKE-AHEAD TIP Fill mushroom caps and refrigerate in airtight container for up to 24 hours before baking.

Per 2 Mushrooms

Calories 120
Fat 10 g
Cholesterol 13 mg
Sodium 160 mg
Carbohydrate 4 g
Fiber 1 g

Crab-Stuffed Mushrooms

Whether you're hosting a glamorous event or something more casual, these delectable appetizers fit right in. Assemble them ahead of time so they will be ready to bake when you are.

24 large button mushrooms
  (1½-inch diameter)
1 package (8 ounces) cream
  cheese, softened
1 can (6.5 ounces) white crab
  meat, drained and flaked
1 teaspoon Worcestershire
  sauce
½ teaspoon soy sauce
¼ teaspoon garlic powder
3 green onions

Rinse mushrooms and pat dry; remove and discard stems. In medium bowl, stir together cream cheese, crab, Worcestershire, soy sauce, and garlic powder. Thinly slice green portion of green onions; set aside for garnish. Slice white portion; stir into crab mixture. Spoon into mushroom caps. Place mushrooms on parchment-lined jellyroll pan. Bake in 350°F. oven until heated through, about 12 to 15 minutes. Place on serving platter; garnish with reserved green onions.

Makes 2 dozen

MAKE-AHEAD TIP Fill mushroom caps and refrigerate in airtight container for up to 24 hours before baking.

Per 2 Mushrooms

Calories 90
Fat 7 g
Cholesterol 38 mg
Sodium 178 mg
Carbohydrate 2 g
Fiber 1 g

Grilled Asparagus and Portabella Pizzas

Thin, crispy egg roll "crusts" topped with grilled marinated vegetables and two kinds of cheese will be a hit at your next party! This rustic appetizer is from Greg and Sue Dierberg's collection of favorites.

1 pound asparagus, trimmed
4 portabella mushrooms, stemmed and gills removed
1 large sweet onion (Maui, Vidalia, Walla Walla), cut into 6 wedges leaving root end intact
1 cup balsamic vinaigrette dressing
6 egg roll wrappers
Olive oil no-stick cooking spray
6 ounces gouda, smoked gouda, or parrano cheese, shredded (about 1 1/2 cups)
6 tablespoons grated parmesan cheese

Place vegetables in large freezer-weight reclosable plastic bag. Pour dressing over vegetables; seal bag and turn to coat vegetables. Place bag on plate and marinate in refrigerator for at least 4 hours or overnight.

Lightly coat both sides of wrappers with cooking spray; place on parchment-lined baking sheets. Bake in 375°F. oven until lightly browned, about 3 minutes per side. (Watch carefully to prevent overbrowning.)

Remove vegetables from bag; discard marinade. Place vegetables on oiled grid or grill pan over medium-high heat; cover and grill turning occasionally until crisp-tender and lightly charred, about 6 to 8 minutes. Cool slightly. Cut grilled vegetables into bite-size pieces.

Sprinkle half of the gouda over baked crusts; top with vegetable pieces and remaining gouda. Sprinkle parmesan over top. Bake in 375°F. oven until cheese melts, about 5 minutes. Cut each pizza into 4 pieces.

Makes 12 servings

TIP Kraft Classic Balsamic Vinaigrette with Extra Virgin Olive Oil is wonderful in this recipe.

Sharon's PARTY TIP

My son and daughter-in-law, Greg and Susan, absolutely love serving these veggie pizzas. What makes them so different is the thin, crispy crust. Their secret? Egg roll wrappers! They're sturdy enough to hold the toppings, but still light and crunchy. The house smells wonderful, too!

---

ingredient savvy

Asparagus

Always choose firm, bright green asparagus with tightly closed purple-tinted buds. Asparagus can be stored for one to two days in the refrigerator. Stand the bunch upright in a container with about an inch of water, cover the tops with a plastic bag, and refrigerate.

Just before cooking, gently snap each stalk at the bottom. It will break at the very spot where woodiness begins. Rinse under cold water and you're ready to get cooking!

Per serving

Calories 113
Fat 5 g
Cholesterol 19 mg
Sodium 209 mg
Carbohydrate 11 g
Fiber 1 g

Tomato Bacon Mini Tarts

Bacon – need we say more? Dierbergs School of Cooking Manager Sally Bruns combines crisp bacon, tomatoes, and mellow Swiss cheese in tiny puff pastry tarts so you get all of your favorite flavors in one delicious bite.

$1/2$ cup mayonnaise

$1/4$ cup finely chopped green onion

1 clove garlic, minced

1 teaspoon dried basil

$1/2$ teaspoon ground black pepper

8 slices bacon, diced, cooked crisp, and drained

1 medium tomato, seeded and diced

3 ounces ($3/4$ cup) shredded Swiss cheese

1 box (17.3 ounces) frozen puff pastry sheets, thawed in refrigerator overnight

In medium bowl, stir together mayonnaise, green onion, garlic, basil, and pepper. Stir in bacon, tomato, and cheese; set aside.

On lightly floured surface, roll 1 pastry sheet into 12-inch square. Using 3-inch round cookie cutter, cut out fourteen circles. Repeat with remaining pastry sheet. Press puff pastry circles into ungreased mini muffin cups. Place 1 heaping teaspoon filling into each pastry cup. Bake in 375°F. oven until pastry is golden brown and puffed, about 20 to 25 minutes. Place on serving tray; serve warm.

Makes 28 appetizers

Sharon's
PARTY TIP

Who doesn't love a BLT? These are just terrific! Have the filling and unbaked shells in the refrigerator ready to go. Then just pop them into the oven when your guests arrive. Yum!

Stuffed Baby Potatoes

Baby potatoes are perfect for a party pickup – no forks required! Assemble these elegant appetizers the day before your party, then pop them into the oven when guests arrive.

2 bags (24 ounces each) baby potatoes (Dutch yellow, white, red, or a combination)
2 tablespoons vegetable oil
1/2 cup milk
1 to 2 teaspoon coarse salt
3 slices black pepper bacon, finely diced and cooked crisp
2 tablespoons pure maple syrup
Freshly ground black pepper
2 ounces gouda cheese, grated (about 1/2 cup)
1 tablespoon roasted garlic
Snipped fresh chives

Cut each potato in half. (To make potatoes sit flat, trim small amount off bottom of each potato cup.) In medium bowl, toss potatoes with oil. Place on jellyroll pan. Roast in 375°F. oven until tender, about 20 to 25 minutes; cool completely.

Use small melon baller to scoop out center of cooked potatoes and place in medium mixing bowl; set potato shells aside. Beat cooked potato until mashed. Beat in milk and salt until fluffy. Divide into 2 bowls.

In small bowl, stir together bacon, syrup, and pepper; mix into one bowl of mashed potatoes. Stir gouda and garlic into second bowl of mashed potatoes. Spoon each filling into half of the potato shells. (Can be made up to this point, covered, and refrigerated for up to 24 hours.)

Place on baking sheets. Bake in 375°F. oven until heated through, about 6 to 8 minutes. Place on serving platter; garnish with chives.

Makes about 4 dozen

Sharon's

This recipe is fantastic and makes plenty of appetizers for a large party. I have actually used these cute, delicious potatoes with just the roasted garlic and bacon on the dinner plate with an entrée, as well!

PARTY TIP

Southwest Roasted Vegetable Bundles

Set out a tray of crisp pastry pouches filled with chile-roasted vegetables and enjoy the compliments. Chipotles add a touch of smoky heat to the garlicky sauce.

technique savvy

Roasting Peppers

Whether you like bell peppers that are mild or chiles that are wild, roasting them mellows their flavor and brings out their natural sweetness. And it makes it easy to remove the skin which can sometimes be tough and bitter. Here are some easy tips:

• Cut peppers through the stem end in half or in quarters. Place skin-side up on foil-lined jellyroll pan.

• Broil peppers 4 inches from heat source until skins turn black and blister, about 5 minutes.

• Gather up edges of foil and seal to form packet.

• Let peppers stand until cool enough to handle, about 10 minutes.

• Gently slip skins off peppers. Remove stems and seeds, and cut as desired.

Per Bundle without Aïoli

Calories 37
Fat 1 g
Cholesterol 0 mg
Sodium 71 mg
Carbohydrate 7 g
Fiber 1 g

1 cup frozen corn, thawed and drained
1 red bell pepper, quartered, seeded, and diced
1 pasilla (poblano) pepper, quartered, seeded, and diced
2 teaspoons olive oil
1 1/2 teaspoons chili powder
1/2 teaspoon salt
1/2 cup black beans, rinsed and drained
8 ounces (1/2 of 16-ounce twin package) frozen fillo dough, thawed in refrigerator overnight
Butter flavor no-stick cooking spray
Chipotle Aïoli

Place corn, bell pepper, and pasilla pepper on foil-lined jellyroll pan that has been lightly coated with no-stick cooking spray. Drizzle olive oil over vegetables and sprinkle with chili powder and salt; toss to coat. Arrange vegetables in single layer. Roast in 425°F. oven stirring once until lightly browned, about 20 to 25 minutes. In medium bowl, combine black beans with roasted vegetables; set aside.

Unroll fillo onto work surface. Cover completely with plastic wrap. Place 1 sheet fillo on clean dry surface; coat with cooking spray. Top with 3 fillo sheets, coating each sheet with cooking spray. Using sharp knife, cut into six 4-inch squares; discard excess fillo. Place 1 tablespoon vegetable filling in center of each square. Bring up 4 corners of fillo; gently pinch together to seal. Place on parchment-lined baking sheet. Repeat with remaining fillo, cooking spray, and filling.

Lightly coat bundles with cooking spray. Bake in 350°F. oven until crisp and golden brown, about 18 to 20 minutes. Place bowl of Chipotle Aïoli on serving platter; arrange bundles around Aïoli.

Makes 30 appetizers

Chipotle Aïoli

1 cup mayonnaise
1 teaspoon chili powder
1 teaspoon chipotle purée
2 cloves garlic, minced

In small bowl, combine all ingredients. Cover and chill at least 1 hour to develop flavors.

Makes 1 cup

Per 2 tablespoons Calories 183; Fat 20 g; Cholesterol 10 mg; Sodium 186 mg; Carbohydrate <1 g; Fiber <1 g

TIP Purchase chipotles in adobo sauce in the Mexican aisle. Purée the chiles with the sauce. Place extra purée in a freezer-weight reclosable plastic bag. Lay flat and freeze. Break off a piece as needed to add a touch of smoky heat to all sorts of dishes.

Mediterranean Feta Bites

These salty, cheesy, crispy appetizers are perfect with cocktails. Keep a supply of unbaked ones in the freezer to bake at a moment's notice.

2 jars (5.75 ounces each) pimiento-stuffed green olives, drained and chopped
2 packages (4 ounces each) crumbled feta cheese
1 cup walnut halves, toasted and coarsely chopped
1 teaspoon ground cumin
1 teaspoon dried oregano
1/2 teaspoon crushed red pepper flakes
1 twin package (16 ounces) frozen fillo dough, thawed in refrigerator overnight
Olive oil no-stick cooking spray
Chopped fresh parsley

In large bowl, combine olives, feta, walnuts, cumin, oregano, and red pepper flakes; set aside.

Unroll fillo onto work surface. Cover completely with plastic wrap. Place 1 sheet fillo on clean dry surface; coat with cooking spray. Top with 2 fillo sheets, coating each sheet with cooking spray.

Spread about 1/3 cup filling down one long side of fillo, about 2 inches from edge. Fold fillo over filling; roll up tightly. Lightly coat with cooking spray. Cut diagonally into 4 pieces. Place seam-side down on parchment-lined baking sheet. Repeat with remaining fillo and filling. Bake in 400°F. oven until crisp and golden brown, about 10 minutes. Place on platter; garnish with chopped parsley.

Makes 4 dozen

Per 2 appetizers

Calories 140
Fat 8 g
Cholesterol 7 mg
Sodium 484 mg
Carbohydrate 14 g
Fiber 1 g

Lemony Olive Medley

Marinate a bowl of colorful olives with a splash of citrus and a sprinkle of fragrant herbs and you're ready to entertain anytime. Serve the olives at room temperature to enjoy their full flavor.

1 pound (2 1/2 cups) assorted pitted olives (ripe, green, kalamata), drained
1 teaspoon grated lemon peel
1 tablespoon fresh lemon juice
1 clove garlic, minced
1/4 teaspoon dried oregano
1/4 teaspoon dried thyme
1/4 cup extra virgin olive oil
Fresh oregano and thyme sprigs

Place olives in large freezer-weight reclosable plastic bag. In small bowl, whisk together lemon peel and juice, garlic, oregano, and thyme. Whisking vigorously, add olive oil in slow, steady stream. Pour mixture over olives; seal bag and turn to coat olives. Place bag on plate and marinate several hours or overnight. Place olives in serving bowl; garnish with oregano and thyme sprigs.

Makes 2 1/2 cups

Per 2 tablespoons

Calories 64
Fat 7 g
Cholesterol 0 mg
Sodium 302 mg
Carbohydrate 1 g
Fiber 1 g

Mini Greek Appetizer Strudels

Filled with savory hummus, roasted sweet peppers, and tangy feta, these hearty strudels make a delicious small plate appetizer.

1 package (10 ounces)
   frozen chopped spinach,
   thawed and well drained
1 cup chopped roasted red
   bell pepper, drained
1 ounce (1/4 cup) crumbled
   feta cheese
1/4 cup pine nuts, toasted
1/4 teaspoon dried oregano
1 sheet (1/2 of 17.3-ounce
   box) frozen puff pastry,
   thawed in refrigerator
   overnight
1 egg, beaten with
   1 tablespoon water
4 tablespoons prepared
   hummus
Fresh oregano sprigs

In medium bowl, combine spinach, roasted bell pepper, feta, pine nuts, and oregano; set aside.

On lightly floured surface, roll pastry sheet into 14-inch square. Cut into four 7-inch squares; brush each square with egg mixture. Spread 1 tablespoon hummus down center of each square leaving 1/2-inch border on each end. Place one-fourth of the spinach mixture down center of each square on top of hummus. **1** Using sharp knife, make cuts 1/2 inch apart down both sides of pastry from filling to edge. **2** Fold pastry strips at an angle across filling, alternating from side to side, to give braided appearance. Fold ends under to enclose filling.

Place on parchment-lined baking sheet; brush top of each strudel with egg mixture. Bake in 400°F. oven until pastry is golden brown and puffed, about 12 to 14 minutes. Cool slightly before cutting each strudel crosswise into 6 pieces. Serve on small plates; garnish with fresh oregano sprigs.

Makes 12 servings

technique savvy

Step-by-Step Instructions

Sharon's

PARTY TIP

I like to serve at least one "high impact" recipe at a party – one that everyone will be talking about the next day. These little strudels are impressively pretty and delicious!

Per serving

Calories 130
Fat 9 g
Cholesterol 20 mg
Sodium 214 mg
Carbohydrate 9 g
Fiber 1 g

Fruit, Glorious Fruit!

Nothing appeals to the senses like a bountiful display of lush, juicy, fresh fruit. All of those wonderful aromas and sweet, tangy flavors – who can resist? Whether you create a display on the grandest of scales or keep things simple, just remember two things – choose in-season fruit and let it ripen. After that, it's all about arranging. Add a fabulous dip to your tray or let the fruit stand on its own for a simple and refreshing appetizer.

Choose Fresh…and Keep It That Way

- Fruit may be cut several hours in advance, but chill each variety in separate containers so flavors don't mingle.

- Prevent apples, bananas, nectarines, peaches, and pears from browning with a splash of lemon-lime soda. The acid keeps the fruit from turning dark too quickly and doesn't interfere with the flavors.

- Rinse strawberries with the caps on so they don't get waterlogged. Rinse all berries just before serving to keep their firm texture.

Get The Look

- For perfectly round melon balls, cut melons in half and remove the seeds. Push the melon baller straight into the melon and twist.

- Leave the rind on melons for a change of pace. Rinse melons thoroughly before cutting. Cut melon into quarters, remove the seeds, and slice them 1/4-inch thick.

- Cut pineapple, mangoes, and papayas into spears for a fresh look.

Razzle Dazzle 'Em

- Cut bunches of grapes into small clusters before placing on the tray so guests can easily serve themselves.

- Add a little height to the platter. Choose one fruit – small clusters of grapes, wedges of melon, or pineapple spears – and pile it up. Stagger other fruits at different levels to keep it interesting. Add height with cake stands.

- Skewer fruit onto decorative wooden picks and fan them out on a platter. Place a bowl of dip in the center for a traditional look or off to one side for a casual look.

- Go for a royal color palette with an arrangement of berries and grapes in shades of red, purple, and blue. Or make a cool and refreshing combination with white grapes, honeydew cubes, and kiwi slices.

---

technique savvy

Fresh Pineapple

Juicy, fresh pineapple is a refreshing addition to any fruit tray. It's easy to cut and enjoy when you have a few helpful tips.

- Choose a pineapple that's fragrant and has skin with a golden undertone.

- Rinse the pineapple, lay on its side, and use a sharp knife to cut off the top.

- Cut pineapple vertically in half and then quarters.

- Trim away the core. Leave the skin on and slice it 1/4- to 1/2-inch thick for a colorful presentation.

- Or remove the skin with a boning knife and cut the pineapple into slices, cubes, or spears.

dips & nibbles

Hot 'n Creamy Crab Dip
Recipe on page 66

Crispy Tortilla Chips
Recipe on page 75

Hot 'n Creamy Crab Dip

A layer of zesty parmesan cheese bakes to golden brown perfection atop this simply divine dip.

Per 2 tablespoons

Calories 73
Fat 6 g
Cholesterol 31 mg
Sodium 170 mg
Carbohydrate 1 g
Fiber <1 g

1 package (8 ounces) cream cheese, softened
1 can (6.5 ounces) white crab meat, drained and flaked
1/4 cup dairy sour cream
1/4 cup finely chopped red bell pepper
2 tablespoons minced shallot
1/2 teaspoon garlic salt
1/2 teaspoon hot pepper sauce
1/4 cup grated parmesan cheese
2 tablespoon snipped fresh chives
Crispy Tortilla Chips (recipe on page 75)

In medium bowl, stir together cream cheese, crab, sour cream, bell pepper, shallot, garlic salt, and hot pepper sauce. Spread in 9-inch glass pie plate or shallow baking dish that has been lightly coated with no-stick cooking spray. Sprinkle parmesan over top. Bake in 350°F. oven until heated through, about 20 minutes. Garnish with chives. Serve warm with Crispy Tortilla Chips.

Makes about 2 cups

Baked Fresh Asparagus Dip

A basket of crisp crackers or chips and a few hungry friends are all you need to enjoy this rich, creamy dip from Laura Dierberg Padousis. Laura suggests it works great to use light cream cheese and reduced-fat mayonnaise.

Per 2 tablespoons

Calories 65
Fat 6 g
Cholesterol 13 mg
Sodium 110 mg
Carbohydrate 1 g
Fiber <1 g

1 pound asparagus, trimmed and sliced 1/4-inch thick
1 1/2 cups (5 ounces) shredded asiago, parmesan, romano cheese blend (divided)
1 package (8 ounces) cream cheese, softened
1/2 cup mayonnaise
1/2 teaspoon herbes de Provence
Freshly ground black pepper
Won Ton Parmesan Crisps (recipe on page 74)

Place asparagus in microwave-safe bowl. Microwave (high) until tender, about 4 to 5 minutes. Cool slightly; drain.

Reserve 1/2 cup cheese blend. In medium bowl, stir together remaining 1 cup cheese blend, cream cheese, mayonnaise, herbes, and pepper. Gently stir in asparagus. Place in 9-inch glass pie plate or shallow baking dish that has been lightly coated with no-stick cooking spray. Sprinkle reserved cheese over top. Bake in 350°F. oven until bubbly and lightly browned, about 20 to 25 minutes. Serve with Won Ton Parmesan Crisps.

Makes about 4 cups

Mia's Bean Dip

Sharing great food – and great recipes – is what entertaining is all about. Greg and Sue Dierberg love this hearty baked dip they enjoyed at a friend's party and now it's on their list of favorites.

1 container (9 ounces) Fritos Mild Bean Dip
1 package (8 ounces) cream cheese, softened
1 container (8 ounces) dairy sour cream
1 package (1 ounce) mild taco seasoning mix
12 drops hot pepper sauce
1 bunch green onions, finely chopped (white portion only)
6 ounces (1½ cups) shredded monterey jack cheese
Tostitos Scoops

In medium bowl, stir together bean dip and cream cheese. Stir in sour cream, taco seasoning, and hot pepper sauce. Stir in onions.

Spread mixture in 9-inch glass pie plate or shallow baking dish that has been lightly coated with no-stick cooking spray. Sprinkle shredded cheese over top. Bake in 350°F. oven until heated through and cheese is melted, about 25 to 30 minutes. Serve with Scoops.

Makes about 5 cups

TIP Look for Fritos Bean Dip at Dierbergs in the chip aisle.

Sharon's PARTY TIP

It's so easy to keep the ingredients for this dip on hand. Plus it goes together very quickly, and that makes it great for last-minute parties. Bob and I love this!

ingredient savvy

Lighten Up!

Don't let guilt spoil the fun of a get-together with friends. Better choices can shave extra fat and calories off of many of your favorite appetizers.

• Make your favorite dip with reduced-fat cheese, sour cream, or mayonnaise. For best results, don't use fat-free unless the recipe specifies it.

• Look for reduced-fat, baked, or fat-free chips, pretzels, and crackers. Try our Crispy Tortilla Chips on page 75.

• Serve crisp vegetable dippers for low-calorie color and crunch.

• Sprinkle in lots of personality with herbs, spices, and reduced-sodium seasoning blends instead of more salt.

Per 2 tablespoons

Calories 58
Fat 5 g
Cholesterol 12 mg
Sodium 142 mg
Carbohydrate 2 g
Fiber <1 g

Shoepeg Corn Dip

Is your usual bowl of chips looking for a change of pace dip? Try Greg and Sue Dierberg's favorite combination of sweet corn and two kinds of cheese. Ritz Toasted Chips make great dippers.

1 cup dairy sour cream
1/2 cup mayonnaise
1 tablespoon finely chopped
 onion
1 can (11 ounces) white
 shoepeg corn, drained
4 ounces (1 cup) shredded
 cheddar cheese
1/4 cup grated parmesan
 cheese
Chopped fresh parsley
Ritz Toasted Chips

In medium bowl, stir together sour cream, mayonnaise, and onion. Stir in corn, cheddar, and parmesan. Cover and chill several hours to develop flavors. Place in serving bowl; garnish with parsley. Serve with Toasted Chips.

Makes 3 cups

Layered Southwest Salsa

You'll love all of the flavors and textures in this colorful salsa from Laura Dierberg Padousis. The secret? A drizzle of cumin-spiked vinegar over each layer. Stack it in a glass dish for an eye-catching snack that's filled with nutritious and healthy ingredients.

1/4 cup red wine vinegar
1 teaspoon ground cumin
1 can (15 ounces) black
 beans, rinsed and drained
2 cups frozen corn, thawed
1 cup diced red onion
1 avocado, halved, seeded,
 peeled, and diced
1 1/2 cups diced roma tomato
1/2 cup thinly sliced green
 onion
Baked tortilla chips

In small bowl, stir together vinegar and cumin. In 9-inch glass pie plate or shallow glass serving dish, layer ingredients except tortilla chips in order listed, drizzling some of the vinegar mixture over each layer. Serve with chips.

Makes about 7 1/2 cups

Spinach Artichoke Dip

You don't have to wait for an evening at your favorite restaurant to enjoy this crowd-pleasing party starter. It's hot, delicious, and ready in about 15 minutes.

1 package (4 ounces) crumbled feta cheese (divided)
1 can (14 ounces) artichoke hearts, drained and chopped
1 package (10 ounces) frozen chopped spinach, thawed and drained
1/2 cup mayonnaise
1/2 cup grated parmesan cheese
1 large clove garlic, minced
1 tablespoon lemon juice
1 teaspoon seasoned salt
1/2 teaspoon dried oregano
Herbed Pita Chips (recipe on page 75)

Reserve 1/4 cup of the feta cheese. In medium bowl, stir together remaining feta with remaining ingredients except Chips.

Spoon into 1-quart baking dish that has been lightly coated with no-stick cooking spray. Sprinkle reserved feta over top. Bake in 400°F. oven until bubbly and lightly browned, about 10 to 12 minutes. Serve with Herbed Pita Chips.

Makes 8 servings

Sharon's PARTY TIP

Who doesn't love a good spinach dip? I mix it up a day or two before a party so I can just pop it into the oven when I'm ready. Easy and delicious!

Per 2 tablespoons

Calories 59
Fat 5 g
Cholesterol 7 mg
Sodium 254 mg
Carbohydrate 2 g
Fiber <1 g

Reuben in Rye

Dierbergs Staff Culinary Professional Therese Lewis transforms the great flavors of the classic deli sandwich into a party-sized dip. Tear off pieces of the warm, crusty loaf and dig in!

2 round loaves rye bread
  (16 ounces each)
1 package (8 ounces) cream
  cheese, softened
1 carton (8 ounces) dairy
  sour cream
1 tablespoon minced onion
1 tablespoon ketchup or
  chili sauce
1 tablespoon spicy brown
  mustard
1/2 pound finely chopped
  lean corned beef
1 can (8 ounces) sauerkraut,
  drained
1 package (8 ounces)
  shredded Swiss cheese

1 Invert medium-size bowl on top of bread; use as a guide to cut to within about 1/2 inch from bottom and sides of bread. **2** Lift middle portion of bread out to form shell; cut or tear pieces into bite-size pieces; set aside.

In large microwave-safe bowl, stir together cream cheese, sour cream, onion, ketchup, and mustard until well mixed. Gently stir in corned beef, sauerkraut, and Swiss cheese. Microwave (high) for 5 to 6 minutes stirring twice until mixture reaches 145°F.

Meanwhile, place bread bowl and bread pieces on jellyroll pan. Bake in 350°F. oven to lightly toast bread, about 10 to 15 minutes.

Spoon corned beef mixture into toasted bread bowl. Place bread bowl on serving platter and surround with toasted bread pieces. Serve warm.

Makes 10-12 servings

Sharon's

PARTY TIP

Need to take an appetizer along to a party? This one is easy, delicious, and travels well. Just make the dip and take it in a covered container. Have the rye bread bowl and dippers ready, and you're good to go. Even easier – bake the dip in a pie plate for about 15 to 20 minutes and serve it with cocktail rye bread or rye crackers. Pretty and easy!

Step-by-Step Instructions

Per serving

Calories 406
Fat 20 g
Cholesterol 55 mg
Sodium 951 mg
Carbohydrate 40 g
Fiber 5 g

Caramelized Onion and Gorgonzola Dip

Here is an onion dip for grown-ups! The subtle flavor of gorgonzola is the perfect complement to sweet caramelized onions.

Gorgonzola Cheese

The city of Milan is Italy's fashion hub, and the nearby village of Gorgonzola (Gor-guhn-ZOH-lah) produces its namesake cheese. Creamy sweet gorgonzola is usually aged for four months. Longer aging makes the cheese more pungent and crumbly.

Serve gorgonzola as the Italians do with a glass of red wine, or as dessert with apples, pears, peaches, nectarines, or figs.

You can also crumble it over salads. A combination of baby greens, juicy pears, and crunchy walnuts is the perfect backdrop for the tangy cheese. Or stir it into potatoes, pasta, or risotto for a punch of flavor.

1 tablespoon olive oil
2 cups chopped onion
1 teaspoon sugar
1 package (4 ounces) crumbled gorgonzola cheese
3/4 cup dairy sour cream
3/4 cup mayonnaise
1 tablespoon fresh lemon juice
1 teaspoon Worcestershire sauce
Chopped fresh parsley
Homemade Crostini

In medium skillet, heat olive oil over medium-high heat. Add onion and sugar; cover and cook stirring frequently until onions wilt, about 5 minutes. Reduce heat, uncover, and cook stirring occasionally until onion is golden brown, about 20 to 25 minutes. Remove from heat; cool slightly.

In large bowl, stir together caramelized onion, gorgonzola, sour cream, mayonnaise, lemon juice, and Worcestershire. Cover and chill 2 hours or up to 3 days to develop flavors. Place in serving bowl; garnish with parsley. Serve with Crostini.

Makes about 2 cups

Homemade Crostini

1 loaf (8 ounces) French baguette, thinly sliced
Olive oil no-stick cooking spray
Old Bay seasoning

Place bread slices on parchment-lined baking sheets; lightly coat with cooking spray. Sprinkle seasoning over top. Bake in 400°F. oven until lightly browned, about 4 to 5 minutes. Cool. Store in airtight container at room temperature.

Makes about 2 dozen

Per 3 Crostini Calories 80; Fat 1 g; Cholesterol 0 mg; Sodium 165 mg; Carbohydrate 16 g; Fiber 1 g

Per 2 tablespoons

Calories 128
Fat 12 g
Cholesterol 14 mg
Sodium 166 mg
Carbohydrate 3 g
Fiber 1 g

Blizzard Fruit Dip

Cool and creamy with a hint of citrus, this light and luscious dip adds a nice finishing touch to any fresh fruit tray. The recipe is from Carol Ziemann, Food Stylist for Dierbergs Presents Everybody Cooks TV show and Dierbergs School of Cooking Instructor.

1 container (8 ounces) dairy sour cream
1 carton (6 ounces) low-fat plain yogurt
1/2 cup sugar
1 teaspoon grated orange, lemon, or lime peel
1 tablespoon fresh orange, lemon, or lime juice

In medium bowl, stir together sour cream, yogurt, sugar, orange peel, and orange juice. Cover and chill for several hours for flavors to develop. Place in serving bowl; serve as dip with fresh fruit.

Makes 2 cups

Sharon's

For a change of pace, I like to serve this parfait-style. When I'm hosting a crowd, I layer fresh fruit and dip in clear plastic tumblers and set them on a pretty serving tray for my guests to serve themselves. Quite a treat!

PARTY TIP

technique savvy

Citrus Zest

The *zest*, or colored portion of the peel, contains fragrant oils that add a bright freshness to all sorts of recipes. When a recipe calls for peel and juice, zest the fruit first so it's easier to handle. A box grater works well. A bartender's channel knife will remove peel in narrow strips. A microplane grater, which resembles a carpenter's wood rasp, is especially handy.

Finely grate just the zest, stopping when you reach the white pith beneath, which is bitter. Freeze any extra grated zest so it's ready when you need it.

Zested citrus may be stored in a plastic bag in the refrigerator for several days. Or cut it in half right away and squeeze out the fresh juice.

Per 2 tablespoons

Calories 62
Fat 3 g
Cholesterol 7 mg
Sodium 15 mg
Carbohydrate 8 g
Fiber 0 g

Easy Parmesan Puffs

These terrific little bites from Sharon Dierberg are like the quintessential little black dress – they're just right for any occasion! For a festive touch, top each puff with a slice of green olive or a sprinkle of capers.

6 slices Pepperidge Farm
  Very Thin White bread
1 cup mayonnaise
1/3 cup dried chopped onion
1/2 cup grated parmesan
  cheese

Trim crusts from bread; cut each slice into quarters to make about 1 1/4-inch squares. Place squares on foil-lined baking sheets.

In medium bowl, stir together mayonnaise and dried onion. Spoon 2 teaspoons mayonnaise mixture on each square. Sprinkle parmesan over top. Bake in 350°F. oven until puffed and golden brown, about 12 to 14 minutes. Serve immediately.

Makes 2 dozen

Won Ton Parmesan Crisps

Tired of traditional chips? Take a tip from Sue and Greg Dierberg and toast up a batch of won ton wrappers dusted with parmesan cheese. Then just watch them disappear!

1 package (16 ounces)
  won ton wrappers
Olive oil no-stick cooking
  spray
1 cup grated parmesan
  cheese

Cut won tons in half diagonally to form triangles. Place triangles on parchment-lined baking sheets; lightly coat with cooking spray. Sprinkle parmesan generously over tops. Bake in 350°F. oven until lightly browned, about 7 to 8 minutes. Store in airtight container at room temperature.

Makes about 10 dozen

Crispy Tortilla Chips

Here's a fun idea for your next fiesta from Dierbergs School of Cooking Instructor Linda Walton. Season different colored tortilla triangles with a variety of spices and bake for a colorful medley of crispy chips.

3 sun-dried tomato flour tortillas (8-inch diameter)
3 plain flour tortillas (8-inch diameter)
2 tablespoons vegetable oil
1 teaspoon Key lime juice
1/2 teaspoon ground cumin
1/2 teaspoon reduced-sodium taco seasoning mix

Cut each tortilla into 8 wedges; arrange in single layer on parchment-lined baking sheets. In small bowl, combine oil and lime juice. Divide into 2 small bowls. Add cumin to one bowl and taco seasoning to second bowl. Brush sun-dried tomato tortillas with cumin mixture and brush flour tortillas with taco seasoning mixture. Bake in 350°F. oven until crisp, about 5 to 10 minutes. Store in airtight containers up to 4 days.

Makes 4 dozen

Per 6 Chips

Calories 121
Fat 5 g
Cholesterol 0 mg
Sodium 101 mg
Carbohydrate 18 g
Fiber 1 g

Herbed Pita Chips

Dierbergs School of Cooking Instructor Nancy Raben serves these hearty whole grain chips in class and never fails to get rave reviews. We're sure they'll be a hit at your next party, too!

3 whole wheat pita breads
1/4 cup finely snipped fresh parsley
2 green onions, finely chopped
1 clove garlic, minced
1 teaspoon olive oil
3/4 teaspoon dried basil, crushed
1/2 teaspoon dried rosemary, crushed
Olive oil no-stick cooking spray
2 tablespoons grated parmesan cheese

Split each pita bread in half; place on parchment-lined baking sheet. In small bowl, stir together parsley, green onions, garlic, olive oil, basil, and rosemary; spread over pitas. Lightly coat tops with no-stick cooking spray; sprinkle with parmesan. Cut each pita into 6 wedges. Bake in 350°F. oven until crisp, about 12 minutes. Store in airtight container up to 1 week.

Makes 3 dozen

TIP Just before serving, crisp Pita Chips in 300°F. oven for about 10 minutes.

Per 6 Chips

Calories 103
Fat 2 g
Cholesterol 2 mg
Sodium 198 mg
Carbohydrate 19 g
Fiber 3 g

Rosemary Parmesan Popcorn

Dress up a bowl of fresh hot popcorn with a drizzle of savory butter for a stylish appetizer at a moment's notice. Try the flavored butter over vegetables, grilled steak, or fish, too.

½ cup popcorn kernels
1 to 2 tablespoons vegetable oil
¼ cup butter
1 teaspoon very finely chopped fresh or dried rosemary
1 small clove garlic, minced
2 tablespoons finely grated parmesan cheese
Salt to taste

In large, heavy saucepan, combine popcorn and oil over medium-high heat. Cover and cook shaking pan occasionally until popping stops, about 7 minutes. Place popcorn in serving bowl.

In 1-cup glass measure, combine butter, rosemary, and garlic. Microwave (high) for 30 seconds or until butter melts. Drizzle melted butter over popped corn as desired, tossing until well combined. Sprinkle parmesan and salt over top.

Makes about 12 cups

VARIATION

Smoked Paprika Popcorn Substitute 1 teaspoon smoked paprika and ⅛ teaspoon ground cayenne pepper for the rosemary and garlic. Omit parmesan cheese.

Per 1 cup Calories 78; Fat 6 g; Cholesterol 10 mg; Sodium 2 mg; Carbohydrate 7 g; Fiber 1 g

Per 1 cup

Calories 79
Fat 6 g
Cholesterol 11 mg
Sodium 14 mg
Carbohydrate 6 g
Fiber 1 g

Chipotle Glazed Pecans

These sweet and smoky pecans from Chef Coby Arzola, owner of Agave Mexican Table and Tequileria in St. Louis, are positively addictive. Don't say we didn't warn you!

1 egg white
1 pound pecan halves
½ cup sugar
1 tablespoon chipotle powder

In medium bowl, beat egg white until frothy. Add pecans, sugar, and chipotle powder; toss until pecans are well coated. Place in single layer on parchment-lined jellyroll pan. Bake in 375°F. oven, stirring every 5 minutes, for 15 minutes. Cool completely; break apart any large clusters. Store in airtight container at room temperature.

Makes 1 pound (about 5 cups)

Per ¼ cup

Calories 104
Fat 9 g
Cholesterol 0 mg
Sodium 3 mg
Carbohydrate 7 g
Fiber 1 g

beverages

Papaya Bellinis
Recipe on page 80

Papaya Bellinis

Inspired by the famous Venetian cocktail, we've substituted papaya for the traditional peach nectar for a tropical touch. The original Bellini was made with Prosecco (see sidebar on page 81), but any sparkling wine can be used. Fantastic!

1 bottle (32 ounces) papaya nectar or juice, chilled
2 bottles (750 ml each) extra dry Champagne, chilled

Pour about 1/4 cup nectar into each Champagne flute. Top with Champagne. Serve immediately.

Makes 12-14 servings

Per serving Calories 114; Fat 0 g; Cholesterol 0 mg; Sodium 10 mg; Carbohydrate 12 g; Fiber 0 g

TIP Try inventing your own delicious version with pomegranate, raspberry, or mango juice or nectar topped with a splash of sparkling wine.

Sparkling Cider Spritzers

Greet your guests with this crisp and sparkling refresher. It's the perfect complement to a warm afternoon.

3/4 cup juice (pomegranate juice, cranberry juice, white grape juice), chilled
1 bottle (750 ml) sparkling apple cider, chilled

Pour 3 tablespoons of the juice into each tall glass. Add sparkling cider to fill glass. Serve immediately.

Makes four 8-ounce servings

Per serving Calories 137; Fat 0 g; Cholesterol 0 mg; Sodium 2 mg; Carbohydrate 34 g; Fiber 0 g

party savvy

Good Libations

Nothing's worse than a room full of parched party goers! Keep everyone happy – and refreshed – with plenty of beverages throughout the event. And as the responsible host, be sure to have an assortment of non-alcoholic drinks chilled and ready to go.

O.K. So, how much is enough? Check out *Cocktail Party Math* on page 8 to help you estimate the number of beverages and amounts of ice you'll need for your gathering.

Sugar doesn't dissolve well in cold liquids; so for mixing cocktails, use *Simple Syrup* instead of sugar to sweeten drinks. It's simple to make! Just combine 2 cups water with 1 cup sugar in a small saucepan and bring it to a boil. Cook 5 minutes or until sugar dissolves. Cool and store in the refrigerator for up to 1 week.

Classic Champagne Punch

Toast any season with a cup of cheer. It's bubbly, refreshing, and not too sweet.

1 bottle (750 ml) pink
 Champagne, chilled
1 bottle (750 ml) blush wine
 (white zinfandel or blush
 chablis), chilled
3 cans (12 ounces each)
 lemon-lime soda, chilled
1/4 cup fresh lemon juice,
 chilled
1/4 cup sugar
Lemon slices
Lime slices

Just before serving, combine Champagne, wine, soda, lemon juice, and sugar in 3-quart punch bowl; stir briskly until sugar dissolves. Float lemon and lime slices on top.

Makes 2 1/2 quarts (twenty 4-ounce servings)

Per serving Calories 83; Fat 0 g; Cholesterol 0 mg; Sodium 5 mg; Carbohydrate 9 g; Fiber 0 g

Hospitality Punch

Dierbergs former Test Kitchen Manager Karen Hurych loves this party-size punch for all kinds of gatherings. Pop it in the freezer for a delicious slush.

1 can (12 ounces) frozen
 pineapple-orange juice
 concentrate, thawed
6 ounces (1/2 of 12-ounce
 can) frozen limeade
 concentrate, thawed
6 ounces (1/2 of 12-ounce
 can) frozen lemonade
 concentrate, thawed
2 cups cold water
1 1/2 cups light rum (optional)
1/2 cup grenadine syrup
1 bottle (2 liters) lemon-lime
 soda or sparkling water,
 chilled
Orange slices

In 2-quart pitcher, combine juice concentrates, water, rum, and grenadine; stir briskly to combine. Chill. Just before serving, pour juice mixture into 4-quart punch bowl; add soda. Float orange slices on top.

Makes about 3 3/4 quarts (about thirty 4-ounce servings)

Per serving with rum Calories 116; Fat 0 g; Cholesterol 0 mg; Sodium 13 mg; Carbohydrate 23 g; Fiber 0 g

Per serving without rum Calories 97; Fat 0 g; Cholesterol 0 mg; Sodium 13 mg; Carbohydrate 25 g; Fiber 0 g

ingredient savvy

Champagne

French monk and cellar master Dom Perignon perfected the technique of fermenting wine in the bottle to produce natural carbonation in the 17th century. This *methode champenoise* (may-TOHD champ-en-WAHZ) is the benchmark for making the most famous sparkling wines in the world!

Champagne is produced only in the Champagne region of France by *methode champenoise.*

Sparkling Wine is made anywhere other than the Champagne region.

Prosecco is Italy's famous dry sparkling wine made from grapes of the same name.

Spumante is an Italian sparkling wine that ranges from dry to sweet, with Asti Spumante being the sweetest.

Brut ....Extra Dry
Extra Dry/Extra Sec ......Dry
Sec ....Semi-sweet
Demi Sec....................Sweet

White Zinfandel Lemonade Slush

When Cookbook Project Manager Janice Martin created this cool and fruity slush for a family get-together, everyone insisted that she share her secret recipe. It's just too good to keep to yourself!

1 bottle (750 ml) white zinfandel, chilled
3 cups cold water
1 can (12 ounces) frozen raspberry lemonade concentrate, thawed
1 cup lemon-flavored vodka
3/4 cup sugar
Fresh raspberries
Lemon slices

In 3-quart freezer container, combine all ingredients except raspberries and lemon slices; stir briskly until sugar dissolves. Cover and freeze stirring occasionally until slushy, at least 24 hours. To serve, spoon slush into wine glasses. Garnish each glass with raspberry and lemon slice. Serve immediately.

Makes about 2 1/2 quarts (twelve 6-ounce servings)

Per serving Calories 192; Fat 0 g; Cholesterol 0 mg; Sodium 9 mg; Carbohydrate 28 g; Fiber 0 g

TIP This is also delicious served as a punch.

Category 5 Slush

Put the freeze on New Orleans' famous Hurricane cocktail and let the good times roll! It's frosty, fruity, and great for serving a crowd.

2 cups orange juice
2 cups pineapple juice
1 cup dark rum
1/2 cup peach-flavored schnapps
1/4 cup grenadine syrup
2 tablespoons fresh lime juice
Ginger ale, chilled
Maraschino cherries with stems

In 2-quart freezer container, combine all ingredients except ginger ale and cherries. Cover and freeze stirring occasionally until slushy, at least 24 hours. To serve, spoon slush into wine glasses, filling two-thirds full. Top with ginger ale and garnish each with a cherry. Serve immediately.

Makes about 2 quarts (ten 6-ounce servings)

Per serving Calories 164; Fat <1 g; Cholesterol 0 mg; Sodium 6 mg; Carbohydrate 22 g; Fiber <1 g

Hot Cranberry Cider

Here's a warm welcome for open-house guests or the sledding crowd. Keep it warm in a slow cooker or coffee carafe and let everyone help themselves.

1 bottle (64 ounces)
   cranberry juice cocktail
1 bottle (64 ounces) apple
   cider
1 bottle (46 ounces) white
   grape juice
4 sticks cinnamon
1 tablespoon whole allspice
1½ teaspoons whole cloves
1 apple, cored and thinly
   sliced

In large non-reactive stockpot, combine all ingredients except apple slices. Bring to a boil over medium-high heat; reduce heat and simmer for 20 to 25 minutes. Remove spices. Ladle into mugs. Garnish each mug with apple slice.

Makes 5 quarts (twenty-five 6-ounce servings)

Per serving Calories 108; Fat 0 g; Cholesterol 0 mg; Sodium 18 mg; Carbohydrate 27 g; Fiber <1 g

TIP Place all ingredients except apple slices in a slow cooker on high heat setting for 1½ hours. Reduce to low heat setting to serve.

Coffee Alexander

Transform your usual cup of coffee into a luscious after-dinner treat. It's wonderful with dessert...or all by itself for dessert!

6 cups hot brewed coffee
3 tablespoons brandy
3 tablespoons crème de cacao
Sweetened softly whipped
   cream

Pour coffee into carafe or thermal pot. Add brandy and crème de cacao. Pour into cups; float thin layer of whipped cream on top. Serve immediately.

Makes 1½ quarts (eight 6-ounce servings)

Per serving with 1 tablespoon whipped cream Calories 62; Fat 3 g; Cholesterol 10 mg; Sodium 7 mg; Carbohydrate 4 g; Fiber 0 g

cuisine savvy

Coffee Bar

Here's a simple party idea: Set out the ingredients along with a *recipe* for a couple variations to make a self-serve coffee bar. Each drink starts with 6 ounces of freshly brewed regular or decaf coffee and is topped off with softly whipped cream.

Irish Coffee
Stir in 2 tablespoons Irish whiskey plus 1 teaspoon brown sugar. Garnish with chocolate shavings.

Jamaican Coffee
Stir in 1 tablespoon coffee liqueur and 1 tablespoon rum. Garnish with dusting of cinnamon.

Café a l'Orange Coffee
Stir in 2 teaspoons orange liqueur. Garnish with strips of orange peel.

Café Chocolate Coffee
Stir in 1 to 2 tablespoons chocolate syrup. Garnish with dusting of cocoa.

desserts

Mini Lemon Cheesecakes
Recipe on page 86

Mini Lemon Cheesecakes

Always include a little something sweet at your appetizer party. Dierbergs School of Cooking Manager Loretta Evans created these bite-size creamy cheesecakes kissed with lemon. They're just the right size for guests to serve themselves.

1¼ cups flour
½ teaspoon baking powder
¼ teaspoon salt
1 cup granulated sugar (divided)
¼ cup butter, softened
2 eggs (divided)
1 teaspoon lemon extract
1 package (8 ounces) light cream cheese, softened
1 teaspoon grated lemon peel
1 teaspoon fresh lemon juice
¼ cup lemon curd
Assorted fresh fruit
Fresh mint sprigs
Powdered sugar

In medium bowl, whisk together flour, baking powder, and salt; set aside.

In large mixer bowl, beat ½ cup of the granulated sugar and butter at medium speed until light and fluffy. Beat in 1 egg and extract. Add flour mixture; beat at low speed until combined. Divide dough among 24 mini muffin cups that have been lightly coated with no-stick cooking spray; press into bottom and up sides of cups. Set aside.

In work bowl of food processor fitted with steel knife blade, combine cream cheese, the remaining ½ cup granulated sugar, the remaining egg, and lemon peel and juice; process until smooth, scraping bowl occasionally. Divide filling evenly among prepared cups. Bake in 350°F. oven until edges are lightly browned and filling is set, about 20 to 22 minutes. Remove mini cheesecakes from pan; cool on wire rack. Place in covered container; chill several hours or overnight.

Spoon ½ teaspoon lemon curd on each cup. Arrange on cake stand; garnish with fruit and mint sprigs, and dust with powdered sugar.

Makes 2 dozen

Sharon's

These make quite an impression when you decorate them with a few berries. Blueberries, raspberries, and blackberries look really pretty together.

PARTY TIP

Piña Colada Cheesecake Bars

If you like piña coladas, you'll love the blend of pineapple, coconut, and a whisper of rum in these delectable bars.

1¼ cups graham cracker
  crumbs
½ cup sweetened flaked
  coconut, toasted
½ cup chopped macadamia
  nuts or walnuts, toasted
¼ cup firmly packed brown
  sugar
¼ cup butter, melted
1 can (8 ounces) crushed
  pineapple in juice
2 packages (8 ounces each)
  cream cheese, softened
1 can (15 ounces) cream of
  coconut
2 tablespoons dark rum, OR
  2 teaspoons rum extract
3 eggs, lightly beaten
1 carton (8 ounces) dairy
  sour cream, at room
  temperature
2 tablespoons granulated
  sugar
1 teaspoon cornstarch
Fresh mint sprigs

Line 9 x 13-inch baking pan with foil (see sidebar). Lightly coat with no-stick cooking spray; set aside.

In medium bowl, combine graham cracker crumbs, coconut, nuts, brown sugar, and butter. Pat into bottom of prepared pan; set aside.

Drain pineapple reserving ¼ cup juice; reserve pineapple for topping. In large mixer bowl, beat cream cheese at medium speed until smooth. Beat in cream of coconut, the ¼ cup pineapple juice, and rum, scraping bowl occasionally until well mixed. With mixer at low speed, beat in eggs, one at a time, just until blended. Pour into prepared crust. Bake in 325°F. oven until center is almost set, about 30 to 35 minutes. Place on wire rack; let stand 10 minutes. Stir sour cream until smooth; spread over top of cheesecake. Bake for 10 minutes. Cool on wire rack to room temperature.

Meanwhile, in 2-cup glass measure, combine reserved pineapple, granulated sugar, and cornstarch. Microwave (high) for 2 minutes stirring once, or until thickened. Cool completely. Spread over sour cream. Chill several hours or overnight before cutting into 2-inch bars. Arrange on serving plate; garnish with mint sprigs.

Makes 2 dozen

Sharon's

The island flavors in these cheesecake bars are terrific – just the thing for a backyard luau! I like to arrange a few palm fronds or banana leaves on the serving table, then put a colorful platter of these bars on top for a tropical look.

PARTY TIP

Per Bar

Calories 205
Fat 15 g
Cholesterol 57 mg
Sodium 159 mg
Carbohydrate 14 g
Fiber 1 g

Chocolate Bourbon Pecan Pies

Dierbergs School of Cooking Manager Ginger Gall created these mini delights as an homage to Southern hospitality. A splash of Kentucky's favorite spirit makes these perfect for entertaining.

1 package (15 ounces) refrigerated pie crust
3/4 cup firmly packed brown sugar
3/4 cup light corn syrup
1/2 cup butter
4 eggs, well beaten
1/4 cup bourbon or coffee-flavored liqueur (Kahlua)
1 teaspoon vanilla extract
1/4 teaspoon salt
1 package (11.5 ounces) bittersweet chocolate chips (divided)
1 package (6 ounces) pecan halves, coarsely chopped

Unroll pie crusts onto lightly floured surface. Lightly roll each pie crust into 12-inch circle. Using 4-inch round cookie cutter, cut 9 rounds from each pastry. (Reroll scraps if needed.) Press each round firmly against bottom and all the way up sides of 18 muffin cups that have been lightly coated with no-stick cooking spray; set aside.

In medium microwave-safe bowl, combine brown sugar, corn syrup, and butter. Microwave (high) 2 to 3 minutes stirring once, or until butter is melted and sugar is dissolved. Cool slightly.

In large bowl, whisk together eggs, bourbon, vanilla, and salt. Slowly whisk in brown sugar mixture. Stir in 1 1/4 cups of the chocolate chips and the pecans. Spoon into prepared crusts, filling about two-thirds full (do not overfill). Sprinkle remaining chocolate chips over top of each pie. Bake in 350°F. oven until set and golden brown, about 20 to 25 minutes. Cool in pans on wire racks. Store at room temperature. To serve, arrange on cake stand.

Makes 18 pies

Per Pie

Calories 391
Fat 27 g
Cholesterol 63 mg
Sodium 154 mg
Carbohydrate 37 g
Fiber 2 g

Chocolate Nut Fillo Pencils

A simple scoop of ice cream becomes a designer dessert when you tuck in one of these crisp chocolate-covered pirouette cookies. Make them ahead, then stash them in a single layer in an airtight container until serving time.

Step-by-Step Instructions

8 ounces (¹/₂ of 16-ounce twin package) frozen fillo dough, thawed in refrigerator overnight

6 tablespoons butter, melted, or butter flavor no-stick cooking spray

¹/₂ cup semisweet chocolate chips

1 teaspoon solid shortening

¹/₄ cup finely chopped almonds

Unroll 12 sheets fillo onto work surface; cover completely with plastic wrap. (Rewrap and refreeze remaining fillo for another use.) Place 1 sheet fillo on clean dry surface; brush with butter or coat with cooking spray. Fold in half crosswise. **1** Starting at folded edge, tightly roll up fillo to form pencil shape. Cut into 3-inch pieces. Place on parchment-lined baking sheet; brush with butter. Repeat with remaining fillo and butter. Bake in 375°F. oven until crispy and golden brown, about 8 minutes. Cool on wire racks.

Place chocolate chips and shortening in small freezer-weight reclosable plastic bag; seal bag. Immerse bag in bowl of very hot water until melted; wipe bag dry. Knead chocolate in bag until completely smooth. Snip off one corner of bag to make small hole. **2** Drizzle chocolate over fillo pencils; sprinkle with almonds. Chill until ready to serve. Arrange on serving tray.

Makes 3 dozen

Sharon's

When you're having a stand-up party, these are the perfect dessert. They're easy to make, serve, and eat, and they're delicious!

PARTY TIP

Per 2 Fillo Pencils

Calories 114

Fat 7 g

Cholesterol 10 mg

Sodium 51 mg

Carbohydrate 13 g

Fiber 1 g

Black and White Mini Cream Puffs

Leave a lasting impression with these elegant little make-ahead puffs drizzled with two kinds of chocolate.

t e c h n i q u e   s a v v y

Cream Puffs

These light and elegant puffs add instant *glam* to any appetizer or dessert tray. But what surprises people the most is how easy they are to make!

Pâte à choux (paht-a-SHOO) or cream puff pastry, bakes into crisp, airy mounds. Cream puff dough starts out on top of the stove and gets a lift from steam that forms when the pastries bake.

Since the flavor is neither sweet nor savory, you can fill them with whatever you like! Best of all, you can freeze the baked, unfilled puffs to enjoy later. Just a few minutes in a hot oven restores their light, crisp texture.

1 cup water
1/2 cup butter
1 cup flour
1/8 teaspoon salt
4 eggs
1 package (4-servings) instant white chocolate pudding mix
2 cups heavy whipping cream
1/4 cup milk
1 teaspoon almond extract
1/3 cup semisweet chocolate chips
1/3 cup white baking chips
1 teaspoon solid shortening (divided)

In medium saucepan, bring water to a boil over medium-high heat. Add butter and cook until melted. Add flour and salt all at once, stirring vigorously until well mixed. Cook over medium-high heat stirring constantly until mixture forms smooth dough that holds together. Remove from heat; cool 10 minutes.

Transfer mixture to work bowl of food processor fitted with steel knife blade. Add eggs, one at a time, through feed tube, processing for 30 seconds after each addition. Drop by heaping teaspoonfuls about 2 inches apart onto parchment-lined baking sheets. Bake in 400°F. oven until golden brown, about 20 to 25 minutes. (Do not open oven door during baking.) Cool puffs on wire racks. Split each cream puff in half and remove any soft dough inside.

In medium mixing bowl, beat pudding mix, cream, milk, and almond extract at medium speed until thick and fluffy, about 2 minutes. Mound filling into bottom of each cream puff and place caps on top.

Place chocolate chips and 1/2 teaspoon of the shortening in small freezer-weight reclosable plastic bag; seal bag. Place white baking chips and the remaining 1/2 teaspoon shortening in another small freezer-weight reclosable plastic bag; seal bag. Immerse both bags in bowl of very hot water until melted; wipe bags dry. Knead chocolate in bags until completely smooth. Snip off one corner of each bag to make small hole; drizzle over tops of Cream Puffs. Chill for up to 24 hours. Arrange on cake stand.

Makes about 2 1/2 dozen

Per 2 Cream Puffs

Calories 295
Fat 23 g
Cholesterol 117 mg
Sodium 154 mg
Carbohydrate 20 g
Fiber <1 g

Strawberry Daiquiri Cupcakes

These pretty pink delights are just the thing for a summery luncheon, bridal shower, or get-together with the girls.

Whipped Cream

A dollop of freshly whipped cream is the crowning glory for many desserts. Be sure to choose *heavy cream* or *heavy whipping cream*, which must contain at least 36% butterfat. Anything lower in fat will not whip.

For perfect whipped cream, chill a deep, narrow bowl and beaters until they are icy cold. Beat the cream at low speed and gradually increase to high as it thickens. For the greatest volume, add sugar or flavorings after the cream forms soft peaks.

To avoid overbeating, finish whisking the cream by hand until desired consistency. Once whipped, store tightly covered in the refrigerator for up to 24 hours.

2 teaspoons grated lime peel
2 tablespoons fresh lime juice
2 tablespoons light rum
1 box (18.25 ounces) strawberry supreme cake mix
Daiquiri Whipped Cream
6 fresh strawberries with caps, quartered
Grated lime peel

In 2-cup glass measure, combine lime peel and juice with rum; add water to equal amount called for on cake mix package. Prepare cake mix according to package directions, substituting lime/rum mixture for water. Line 24 muffin cups with paper baking cups. Spoon batter into muffin cups, filling about two-thirds full. Bake in 350°F. oven until wooden pick inserted in center comes out clean, about 15 to 17 minutes. Remove cupcakes from pans; place on wire racks and cool completely.

Spread or pipe Daiquiri Whipped Cream onto cupcakes. Store in refrigerator. Arrange on cake stand; garnish each cupcake with quartered strawberry and grated lime peel.

Makes 2 dozen

Daiquiri Whipped Cream

2 cups 40% gourmet heavy whipping cream
¼ cup powdered sugar
3 tablespoons light rum, OR 1 teaspoon rum extract

In large mixer bowl, beat cream, powdered sugar, and rum at high speed until stiff peaks form. Store in refrigerator.

Makes 4 cups

Per 2 tablespoons Calories 58; Fat 6 g; Cholesterol 21 mg; Sodium 6 mg; Carbohydrate 1 g; Fiber 0 g

Per Cupcake

Calories 206
Fat 13 g
Cholesterol 55 mg
Sodium 153 mg
Carbohydrate 19 g
Fiber <1 g

Sharon's

PARTY TIP

You can make individual cupcake pedestals by turning stemmed glasses upside-down. Try using a variety of heights for a little whimsy.

Nutrition Information

In *Appetizers*, you'll find heart-healthy recipes identified by the red heart logo shown with the nutrition analysis. Dierbergs Markets along with Missouri Baptist Medical Center, a member of BJC HealthCare, proudly sponsor *Eat Hearty®*, an informational program aimed at helping you choose a heart-healthy eating plan. *The program includes a shelf tag program, cooking classes, information on the web, and healthy recipes. For more information visit* **www.dierbergs.com** *or* **www.missouribaptist.org.**

Criteria Used for Calculating Nutrition Information

- Whenever a choice is given, the following are used: The first ingredient; the lesser amount of an ingredient; the larger number of servings.

- Ingredients without specific amounts listed, such as "optional" or "toppings," have not been included in the analysis.

- To qualify for a red heart logo, appetizers must have 3 g fat and 480 mg sodium or less; desserts must have 5 g fat and 480 mg sodium or less; alcoholic beverages have not been evaluated.

- The nutrition information provided in *Appetizers* was calculated using *Nutritionist Pro*, a nutrition analysis program developed by Axxya Systems. The information is believed to be reliable and correct.

- The nutrition professionals compiling the information have made every effort to present the most accurate information available, but have undertaken no independent examination, investigation or verification of information provided by original sources. Therefore, Dierbergs assumes no liability and denies any responsibility for incorrect information resulting from the use of the nutrition information provided in *Appetizers*.

Ingredients Used in Nutrition Calculation

- Certain ingredients are considered "standard" for nutrition analysis. They include large eggs, 2% milk, lean ground beef, and canned broth. Other ingredient selections were based on information from the USDA and/or readily available brands.

- If a recipe specifies reduced-fat/reduced-sodium products in the ingredient list, these products were used for nutrition analysis.

- Some recipes meet *Eat Hearty* criteria without modification. You may wish to make additional substitutions to further reduce the fat/sodium content of these recipes; however, these changes may alter the results of the recipe.

All Foods Can Fit

Serving an appetizer can tantalize the palate and rev the appetite for the upcoming meal. Appetizers can compliment the flavors of the meal and your healthy eating style, too!

Simply go for balance. If your entrée is on the light side, there's room for a bit of decadence in an appetizer. Or if your meal ends with an outrageous dessert, keep the balance with a lighter appetizer.

Many appetizers are party fare to enjoy on special occasions, not routinely. It's your food choices over time that add to a healthy eating style, not just a single food or meal. So enjoy a variety of these bite-sized starters, and you'll find there's always room on your plate for great taste and good nutrition!

Sherri Hoyt, RD, LD
Missouri Baptist Medical Center

Index

♥ Heart Healthy Recipe
◆ Photograph of Recipe
Items in italic are sidebars